The Tao of Writing

Imagine. Create. Flow.

Ralph L. Wahlstrom

Adams Media
Avon, Massachusetts

Published by
Adams Media, an F+W Publications Company
57 Littlefield Street, Avon, MA 02322. U.S.A.
www.adamsmedia.com

ISBN: 1-59337-404-6

Printed in Canada.

J I H G F E D C B A

Library of Congress Cataloging-in-Publication Data
Wahlstrom, Ralph L.
The Tao of writing : imagine, create, flow / Ralph L. Wahlstrom.
p. cm.
Includes bibliographical references.
ISBN 1-59337-404-6
1. Authorship--Philosophy. 2. Authorship--Psychological aspects. I. Title.
PN175.W34 2005
808.001--dc22
2005026449

This publication is designed to provide accurate and authoritative information with regard
to the subject matter covered. It is sold with the understanding that the publisher is not
engaged in rendering legal, accounting, or other professional advice. If legal advice or
other expert assistance is required, the services of a competent professional person should
be sought.

—From a *Declaration of Principles* jointly adopted by a Committee of the
American Bar Association and a Committee of Publishers and Associations

Many of the designations used by manufacturers and sellers to distinguish their
products are claimed as trademarks. Where those designations appear in this book
and Adams Media was aware of a trademark claim, the designations have been
printed in initial capital letters.

This book is available at quantity discounts for bulk purchases.
For information, call 1-800-872-5627.

Contents

vii   Preface

xi   The Beginning

1   Part 1: The Philosophy—Why the Tao in Writing?

     3   My Path to the Tao of Writing

     13   Making Connections: Writing and the Tao

23   Part 2: Twelve Principles of the Tao of Writing

     25   1. Writing is natural

     31   2. Writing is flow

     37   3. Writing is creation

     45   4. Writing is detachment

     61   5. Writing is discovery

     75   6. Writing is change

     85   7. Writing is unified yet multiplied

     93   8. Writing is clarity

     99   9. Writing is simplicity

     105   10. Writing is personal

111   11. Writing is universal
117   12. Writing is open-ended

123   Part 3: Applying the Tao to Writing
      125   Te: The Tao of Writing Is an Ethical Way
      133   The Tao Is a Peaceful Way
      139   The Writing Space
      159   The Writer's Tools
      165   A Final Word

167   Part 4: Writing Activities
203   Bibliography

Dedication

It isn't easy to write a dedication. We are the consequences of countless influences, of being touched by so many people in our lives that it is virtually impossible to do them justice. Then, of course, there is the question of whether or not our work can do them justice. Here goes. First, I dedicate this manuscript to my wife Cynthia, without whom none of this could have happened. I also have to thank Diana George, my teacher, mentor, and friend whose rigorous scholarship and gentle way inspired and guided me through my studies. Thank you, John Kuhn, Dick Carter, and Sister Emerita Joseph. You each lived the Tao in your own way. I am also grateful to my student, Dana, who planted the seed, and to a generous Peter Elbow, who gave it water. Finally, I dedicate this book to my loving parents, Anna and Leroy, whose kindness, generosity, and love are the most profound kind of inspiration.

Preface

Something has happened to me as I've experienced the writing of this book. The project began almost by chance, an interesting idea taken partly from a student paper called "The Tao of Tutoring" and a chalkboard demonstration for one of my writing classes.

I had always found the East fascinating and had been drawn to Taoist philosophy since my teen years. Events and influences accumulated in the ensuing years until that one day when, in an almost offhand way, I found myself writing "The Tao of Writing" across the top of the chalkboard. The idea took root and began to grow. I became so intrigued by the subject, the increasingly clear connections between writing and the Tao, that I kept at it, picking away, adding a little here and there, generally avoiding real work to play at my Tao piece whenever I could manage it. At first I approached it the way I would normally plan and work on most academic writing. I gathered my sources and began plugging things in that seemed to fit, being sure to cite the appropriate experts along the way. Then the whole thing began to shift away from the conventional and rigid form of scholarship to something more personal and, at the same time I think, more universal. I would even dare to say that I began to write in the Tao rather than writing about it.

First, I had to discover why I was writing a book about Taoism—and, in fact, why I was writing at all. I am no great Taoist scholar and, as one scholarly friend once told me, I'm not exactly an intellectual either. So how is it my place to write a book entitled *The Tao of Writing*?

My first instinct was to follow a familiar path, a scholarly format if not a highly intellectual one. But as I read what I wrote, I found I didn't like the parts that discussed composition theory and formal practice. It's what I knew intellectually, but it didn't feel right. What I liked best were the places where I spoke about writing by looking at other things, other parts of life. I found metaphors for the Tao of writing in my music and fiction and, ultimately, in art. My friend was right—I am not an intellectual. I tend to be more in tune with my feelings than with academic theories. I don't give exams in my writing classes, because I believe they have nothing to do with becoming a writer. And although I've spent many years reading current theories on writing and rhetoric, and I enjoy the conversation immensely, I see little use for most of it in a writing classroom. Writing is a combination of sensation, experience, and knowledge.

So, I needed to cut myself free of the restrictions I had imposed on this text. I stopped keeping count of the words I had written up to that point. I was no longer trying to write a book. I was, instead, just writing. I also decided to step away from composition technique and theory, at least as much as seemed reasonable, and to explore other areas that seemed more in tune with the Tao. To that end I picked up books on creativity and flow by Mihaly Csikszentmihalyi and a strange little book called *On Not Being Able to Paint*, written by psychologist Marion Milner in 1957. I found inspiration in one of my favorite books, *A River Runs Through It*, as well as in the writings of Ray Bradbury, the music of James Taylor, and in my long bicycle rides through the hills of rural Western New York. And I returned to a hobby that had been a passion when I was younger, painting and illustration. Over the years, as my painting has become more formal, more structured and bound in technique and form, it's also become boring. This writing, this experience has freed me to again paint and draw without worrying about being right. So, just as I've stopped struggling to get a line or color right, I've stopped counting words, and I'm not concerned that I have to cover the fine points of composition theory.

I'm also not so worried about whether this is a book that will appeal to my friends and colleagues who are or wish to be "intellectuals." The other day I heard a discussion on the radio about J. R. R. Tolkien's *Lord of the Rings* trilogy. The popularity of the remarkable new film versions of the books had raised a lot of interest in the works, so NPR's *Talk of the Nation* had brought a group of well-known authors together to revisit Tolkien's fantasy world. A listener sent the panel a comment in which he called the work dull and intellectually uninteresting. When asked to respond to the criticism, one of the show's guests, author Ursula Le Guin, laughed and said, "I feel sorry for him." Ray Bradbury, one of my favorite writers as I was growing up, writes about the day he stopped worrying about the critics. He was nine years old and had a passion for Buck Rogers comics. When his fourth-grade cronies chided him for reading such childish stuff, he went home and tore his comics to pieces. A month later, the young boy made his choice. He writes, "I went back to collecting Buck Rogers. My life has been happy ever since. For that was the beginning of my writing science fiction. Since then, I have never listened to anyone who criticized my taste in space travel, sideshows, or gorillas. When this occurs, I pack up my dinosaurs and leave the room" (Bradbury, 52). (*Note:* throughout this book, author names and page numbers in parentheses refer to the entries in the Bibliography starting on page 203.)

This book is not about academic theories and exercises, although they have their place in the writer's development and craft. This is about a love for writing and the realization that writing is as much of us as is speaking and walking. The wonderful thing about this manuscript is that I have, less and less, been writing it. It seems to have begun writing me and has given me more than insight into writing. I don't think I'm overstating it to say that this writing has carried me along and given me insight into myself.

The most familiar and quoted Taoist phrase may well be this: "The journey of a thousand miles starts with one step." The writer's journey begins with a word and, like the river and the wind, flows on. This is the Way, the Tao of writing.

The Beginning

In 1983, my wife, Cynthia, my six-month-old son, Erik, and I journeyed to the People's Republic of China so that I could teach writing and so that we could learn more than we ever imagined we would. It was there in the dry, dusty, stiflingly hot or bitterly cold landscape of northwestern China that we discovered the strange contradictions of a changing Communist country and traditional culture—and a Taoist way of existing. We left with a love for the people and a lasting appreciation and wonder at their ability to endure these contradictions and, essentially, to go with the flow.

Just a few years later, I was working as a middle level administrator at a small University of Wisconsin campus. One day, Dick Carter, a supervisor at my work, lent me a copy of a book by John Heider called *The Tao of Leadership*. I was impressed and intrigued by a philosophy that seemed so different from conventional management approaches, one that didn't even seem to be management at all. I made an effort to adopt some of the book's Taoist ideas because they made sense to me.

Still, I didn't recognize the growing influence of this philosophy on me, and I did not consciously follow up on the concept of Taoism until recently, when I met a practitioner of the philosophy and became curious to know more about it. I was reminded of a former student's paper entitled "The Tao of Tutoring."Dana, my student, had explored the interaction between a writing tutor and a student from a loosely Taoist perspective. In general, her paper showed how good student-centered tutoring practice is essentially Taoist in that the effective tutor will "follow the energy of the writer rather than try to divert it." I liked the idea so well that it had stayed in the back of my mind for years.

As a result, these scattered influences began to form a unity that seemed to make sense, not only in philosophical terms, but in practical terms as well. Each of these influences, these brief encounters with Taoist ideas and people, shared much in common. The Chinese culture (though not the government or political system) was to me generous and based on community, a place where people could feel at ease and at peace, where life flowed along as the river flows. My old supervisor also taught me the joys of managing without controlling, of encouraging an atmosphere of community and generosity, of putting daily stresses into perspective. Then, young Dana showed me—or perhaps simply reminded me—that I could think about writing from this new perspective. It was all natural. Because I am a writer and a teacher of writing, and I spend a good deal of time thinking about writing and helping others to become writers, the connections between the Tao and writing started to become more and more apparent to me.

If everything is so natural, though, an essential question arises: "Why is writing so hard?" We look at the writing of great and not-so-great authors and we say, "I wish I could write like that." It's a difficult comparison, and one that can't help our self-esteem. Then we take that insecurity to the next level and convince ourselves that we can't write like that because we are not good writers. Those few among us who think of themselves as competent users of the written word are not much more confident than the majority who simply say, "I can't write." We too struggle for the right word, the right number of pages, and when we finally manage to get words onto paper (or into a computer file) we worry that they are not good enough.

Why is writing so hard? Why does it seem so much more difficult than just about everything else we do? After all, we manage to communicate pretty effectively in other aspects of our lives. We don't spend hours fretting over the word selection, grammar, and thesis when we're at the gym or in a restaurant with friends talking about last night's ball game, the latest CD by a favorite singer, current politics, work, love, family, and life in general. We just do it and it usually works pretty well.

I realize that writing does not have to be the painful experience we seem to believe it to be, and yet, like most people, I go through a cycle of doubt and second-guessing as I write. On the face of it, I have some good reasons for questioning my writing. We in higher education are up against tenure requirements that include a need to publish and write grants. Then, of course, I teach writing, so I should be a great writer, or at least pretty good. The problem is no less serious for most people. Writing a memo, a letter of love, a complaint, or a job application, or simply wanting to set down family stories for posterity—all these give rise to anxiety. Then, because we're worried about our writing (we've spent a good deal of time convincing ourselves that it's lousy) and what people will think, we put it off, struggle and suffer through it, and too often end up not writing at all.

So we worry. Is it even possible for writing to be anxiety-free? Probably not, but in many cases it can be relatively stress-free. Let's be realistic: writing, like the world, like the Tao itself, is created in the opposition of forces. The tension of writing is inevitable, but it also is a great creative force that can contribute to and, ultimately, give way to the flow of the Tao, to the joy that comes from writing.

Part 1

The Philosophy—
Why the Tao in Writing?

My Path to the Tao of Writing

Recently, a friend asked me why I'd bother to write another book about writing. He was right to be skeptical. My shelves are packed with books on writing essays, fiction, and creative nonfiction; writing for the arts/sciences/social sciences; and technical and professional writing. The problem is that most of these books, especially those designed for high school and college writing classes, give essentially the same advice and instruction. It tends to be good advice, but we have heard it over and over again. The problem is not that we don't get the right tips on how to write; we're buried in them. It's more that we have not learned to see the connections between the written word and the world in and around us. We tend not to recognize that the flow of Tao is inherent in how we see, how we interpret, and how we communicate that world. Paulo Freire, the great Brazilian literacy activist, had it right when he told us that the word is the world, and that we learn to read [and write] the word and the world as naturally as we learn to interact with the soil, the sky, and the animals.

The truth is I hadn't planned on writing a book at all. I was simply taken by an idea, which then took hold in my imagination and settled there. Once I began thinking about writing in Taoist terms I began to see clearly the relationship between "the way" described in the Tao Te Ching and the "ways of writing" described by the best writers and teachers of writing.

It is not my intention here to tie anyone to a specific set of rules to writing. It would be impractical and not very Taoist anyway. Even so, the Western approach to Eastern philosophy does not typically follow Eastern practice. We are, it seems, a stubbornly pragmatic people. William James, the philosopher and psychologist, once wrote that "pragmatism always asks, 'What difference would it make in practice?'" (Simpkins, 2). Thus our approach to Buddhism, Taoism, and other esoteric Eastern philosophies tends to demand a usefulness in our lives that is particularly American, not Eastern, and often not so useful as we might think. We look to solve problems and to improve our way of life as we search for answers.

In that spirit, this book is intended to bring certain useful bits and pieces to writing and, more importantly, to becoming a writer. In addition, I confess that the Tao of writing seems to fit my personal philosophy of writing. It just feels like the best interpretation of the best writing advice I've ever gotten—or given. And so, I hope you find it as compelling and worthwhile as I have as we explore the Tao of writing.

Infinite Lines

The Way that can be experienced is not true;
The world that can be constructed is not true.
The Way manifests all that happens and may happen;
The world represents all that exists and may exist.
To experience without intention is to sense the world;
To experience with intention is to anticipate the world.
These two experiences are indistinguishable;
Their construction differs but their effect is the same.
Beyond the gate of experience flows the Way,

Which is ever greater and more subtle than the world.
(Tao Te Ching, verse 1)

Tao means "the Way," and it reflects a particular interpretation of the ways in which the world and the universe work. Douglas Chung describes Taoism as "the cosmic, mysterious, and ultimate principle underlying form, substance, being, and change." It describes a world of balance and flow. What this means to your work, and specifically to how you write, is that the Tao offers principles which can guide writers (and those of us who work with writers) as we compose and develop our writing voices. The Tao offers us the time and space in which to think and write. It gives us a river upon which our writing can flow and describes a framework that is not so much imposed upon us but which is already there in the ways we use language, in the landscape, in the very weave of the universe.

As I think about this, I keep going back to a vivid metaphor found in Carlos Castaneda's *Journey to Ixtlan*. For those unfamiliar with Castaneda's work, *Journey* is part of a series in which he chronicles his spiritual, perhaps even magical, adventures through Mexico and parts of the Southwestern United States. Castaneda describes a place between the physical and metaphysical where he can see the "lines of the world . . . Infinite numbers of lines" (Castaneda, 192) joining us to one another and everything else. It is a web of connections between the physical and metaphysical worlds. Castaneda's lines, like many of his experiences, may have been real, imagined, hallucinatory, or fictional, but they reflect the very real interconnectedness between our inner and outer spaces. Writing is much like the world Castaneda describes. Writing is not separate from the rest of existence. It is as much connected to our breathing and to the wind as it is to the book report Mrs. Peterson assigned in seventh grade. It is linked to the physical spaces in which we operate and to our inner worlds, our unconscious, the metaphysical, and the spiritual. Once we begin to understand this, to see the lines of the writing world and many other worlds as they link, interconnect, and interact, we can begin to write with a natural flow and joy. When we write in this way, joyfully in the current of the Tao, we become better writers. We become truthful writers.

How We Become Writers

This book is directed toward anyone who writes or wishes to write. As I am a writing teacher, though, I should talk for just a moment about the schooling that influences the different ways so many of us become writers.

Traditional writing instruction is the antithesis of the Taoist ideal. It is a painfully rigid, rule-bound system that has teachers and students imposing structure on ideas and forcing topics into structure. An extreme example might be the old practice of requiring students to write an outline then, holding strictly to that framework, to write an essay. This might work if good creative writing emerged whole-cloth from an author's mind, but it doesn't. In fact, writing is nearly always born in the act of writing. Other examples of this constrictive system include things such as teaching grammar—sentence structure, spelling, punctuation, and such—in the guise of writing instruction; focusing on the five-paragraph essay; and grading student work in any number of ways—quantitatively, qualitatively, holistically, or using the Ouija Board. All teachers of English and of writing do this in one way or another, so I'm in no better position than anybody else to accuse or blame. In fact, novice writers probably do benefit from a range of teaching practices in the classroom, and we can certainly all become better writers through using a variety of approaches. No, my intention here is to explore a philosophy of writing that taps each writer's natural flow.

I knew from early on that there had to be better ways of teaching writing and, indeed, of writing. My desire to learn more about writing led me to the Ph.D. program in Rhetoric and Technical Communication at Michigan Technological University and, by virtue of my contact with Diana George, Cynthia Selfe, and others at that snowbound institution, to a broader understanding of what writing is and just how powerful it can be in life and culture. I learned how Paulo Freire saw that illiteracy prevented the Brazilian peasants from being heard, from having a voice in the politics, economy, and culture of their country. When he began his literacy circles in which indigenous peasants learned to read and write through pictures and music, through their own culture, his success so frightened the Brazilian oligarchy that he was exiled. Freire discovered that literacy and culture, when taken together, are a powerful, liberating force. They can free a people politically, and they can free each of us from the bonds that hold us so rigidly in place.

I was captivated by this vision of writing and reading as liberating and natural, and I wanted to find out more, to bring this brave new world into my own practices. My studies brought me through the movements and changes in the ways we approach text from classical rhetoric through the process movement and into postmodernism, that chaos and anti-chaos that so vexes graduate students. It was a complicated and, in a strange way, fun time in my life. A lot of what I was reading was what one of my students recently called "wacko intellectual stuff," but the challenge and the innovative ideas got my blood pumping and my brain working overtime. The combination of graduate school, being a father and husband, and still trying to earn a living was the hardest work I've ever done, and at times I was exhausted, but I threw myself into the flow of the moment and let it carry me along. Ultimately, and just a little naively, I knew that I had found a new life and I began to imagine that I'd found a recipe for writing in the new age.

First, the approach must be liberating in the way Paulo Freire's practices empowered and liberated. Second, it had to be flexible, to fit all kinds of writers—urban, rural, suburban; black, white, Latin, Asian; poor or wealthy. Third, it had to be appealing, to blend pleasure with substance. Finally, it had to be effective.

Novice writers approach the writing task with misgivings about what it means to be a writer. To most of us, writing doesn't mean self-expression; it means following rules. Writing doesn't mean discovery; it means restating old news. It doesn't mean learning and developing a critical sense; it means keeping strictly to well-worn paths and making predictable choices. Finally, it doesn't mean writing for readers. Let's face it: for most of us, school has defined writing as responding to a dull topic with a dull essay. It's all about getting it done, handing it in, and getting a grade. No wonder so many Americans say they hate to write. They've come to believe that writing is a process of arranging chunks—awkward and heavy bricks of a sort—into rigid structures that match the templates in old writing textbooks. The result is that too many of us stumble and trip as we lug about these ponderous chunks of concrete.

By contrast, the Tao, and writing in the Tao, is about flow—the flow of rivers, time, the universe, the flow of words and ideas. As in Buddhism, the Taoist world is in constant influx: growing, changing, corrupting, dying, being reborn; growing, changing, corrupting, dying, being reborn—and then once more growing, changing, corrupting, dying, being reborn, and so on. Yet in this change is the unchanging flow, like a river, always new yet always old, always different yet always the same.

In these pages we will explore the flow of writing, the ways in which the straight-ahead nature of composition melds with the recurring elements of existence—birth, death, and renewal—to inspire and compel writers. Successful writers, those who write well, who experience the power and rhythm of writing, have understood this. Mark Twain, for example, wrote volumes, much of it good, but very little of it great. Yet that small part is profound, and the sum of it all makes for greatness.

Most people in approaching a writing task write against the flow, constantly bumping up against and trying to overcome the rocky rules of writing. They tend to struggle for ideas and words. They think in terms of numbers of words and pages. They toil over the mechanics of writing, syntax, and punctuation. Instead of composing, they seem to construct, feeling that they need to be correct and find each right word before they are able to go on to the next. The result of this obstacle course is that, unlike the prolific authors on our shelves, most of us don't write very much at all. It makes sense. Why write if it's so difficult? Why write when it's so painful?

The Pain of Writing

It is true. Writing can be painful. The Tao acknowledges struggle, pain, and hardship, but it doesn't ask that we volunteer for misery. It offers an opportunity for free, unencumbered flow in writing. We often hear athletes talk about being "in the zone." The great hitter in baseball might claim that the ball seems to slow down as his perception becomes completely absorbed in the moment, and his body and mind, the ball, and the bat are all interconnected in that moment. This might be called the Tao of baseball.

Musicians, dancers, and artists in general can relate a similar experience, one in which time seems to stand still. For years I worked as a professional musician and singer. Most of the time the nights in smoky, crowded hotel bars and clubs were long, hard work. Once in a while, though, I would find myself completely in the music, almost as if it were a dream. The room would disappear, leaving only the music, until I emerged from that "zone" and found myself back in that noisy, smoky bar. In her book *On Not Being Able to Paint*, Marion Milner talks about reaching the "zone" and specifically about a moment when she was able to create after a long drought:

There was also another reason why it was now possible to paint. It was because there was one central fact that made it seem worthwhile going on, whatever the objective value of the pictures to other people. It was that I had discovered in the painting a bit of experience that made all other occupations unimportant by comparison. It was the discovery that, when painting, something from nature there occurred, at least sometimes, a fusion into a never-before-known wholeness; not only were the object and oneself no longer felt to be separate, but neither were thought and sensation and feeling and action towards it, the movement of one's hand together with the feeling of delight in the "thusness" of the thing, they all seemed fused into a wholeness of being which was different than anything else that had ever happened to me (Milner, 142).

This "feeling of thusness" is the zone.

In a recent radio interview, James Taylor talked about this transcendent quality in song writing. He said that when he was writing well, it was almost as if he were channeling the songs. We all know this feeling. Many of us get lost in our hobbies. Craftsmen, carpenters, bricklayers, gardeners, skiers, and, of course, writers all have moments of transcendence. In his book *Zen in the Art of Writing*, Ray Bradbury writes about the first time he found his version of the zone and emerging with "The Lake," a story that virtually finished itself two hours later. Like many writers, I can relate to Bradbury's experiences. I myself have at times written pieces in an almost trance-like state, oblivious to the outside world and the passage of time. At such moments, for the writer, the clatter of the external world gives way to something more, a transcendence. This is the Tao of writing.

Making Connections:
Writing and the Tao

The connections between writing and the Tao have not been completely ignored by popular and scholarly writing experts. Peter Elbow (in *Writing with Power*) and Steven Zemelman and Harvey Daniels (in *A Community of Writers*) have discussed the natural and holistic nature of the writing process. When we recognize that writing and learning to love the act of writing are not the sole property of intellectuals and so-called experts, the ability to write with love and joy is in all of us. As with much in life, when we try to force the writing, we often end up with uninteresting, barren, joyless text; when we tap into the flow, we are likely to find ourselves carried along on a joyful, creative, fulfilling stream. Within this stream are tenets of life that apply readily to the act of writing.

Taoism is a philosophy of creativity, utility, and joy. From this general impression and after reading extensively, I identified twelve principles of the Tao of Writing. In Part 2 of this book, we'll examine the following principles in detail:

1. Writing is natural
2. Writing is flow
3. Writing is creation
4. Writing is detachment
5. Writing is discovery
6. Writing is change

7. Writing is unified yet multiplied
8. Writing is clarity
9. Writing is simplicity
10. Writing is personal
11. Writing is universal
12. Writing is open-ended

The Essence of Tao

The Tao Te Ching is considered by most to present the essence of the Tao. According to tradition, Lao Tzu (a contemporary of Confucius) composed this poetic work in China during the sixth century B.C., though some scholars believe the work may be of later and more complicated origins. In the eighty-one verses (or chapters) of the Tao Te Ching, Lao Tzu (whose name is often translated as "Old Master") is said to have expressed the meaning of existence.

The tenets of the Tao Te Ching, which seem to fit the many concerns of modern societies as they had the old, also have a good deal to contribute to writing teachers and writers. My own early introduction to writing and teaching writing focused on Peter Elbow, Mina Shaughnessy, Paulo Freire, and others who saw literacy in general and writing in particular as an organic process that blended the personal and public, the conventional and innovative. These were the radicals, the out-there crowd in writing programs, and they got my attention. In many cases, as with Freire and Elbow, this melding was almost spiritual, depending on cultural norms, traditions, and beliefs.

The philosophies of these writers are reflected in more current writing instruction and practice and are also mirrored in the Tao. When I first began studying these teachers of writing, I had enough of an understanding of Taoism that my sense of its connection to these writers remained unclear but persistent. The more I read and considered these ideas, the clearer it became. My philosophy of teaching writing is founded on a writer-centered, text and context-based approach that attempts to bridge the contradictions in public and private, school and home literacies, and in the ways we think about drafting and revising text. To put it more simply, I believe we write about what's important to us, and just about everything is important when we see the connections between our personal lives and the rest of the world. The Tao makes these connections explicit.

In "Taoism: A Portrait," Douglas K. Chung defines the philosophy this way: Taoism tells us that the "Tao" is the cosmic, mysterious, and ultimate principle underlying form, substance, being, and change. Tao encompasses everything. It can be used to understand the universe and nature as well as the human body. For example, "Tao gives birth to the One, the One gives birth to Two, and from Two emerges Three, Three gives birth to all the things. All things carry the Yin and the Yang, deriving their vital harmony from the proper blending of the two vital forces" (Tao Te Ching, verse 42). Tao is the cause of change and the source of all nature, including humanity. Everything from quanta to solar systems consists of two primary elements of existence, Yin and Yang forces, which represent all opposites. These two forces are complementary elements in any system and result in the harmony or balance of the system. All systems coexist in an interdependent network. The dynamic tension between Yin and Yang forces in all systems results in an endless process of change: production and reproduction and the transformation of energy. This is the natural order.

This balance of Yin and Yang speaks to the organic nature of writing and the writer as well as to the ideas of creation and revision. Further along, Douglas Chung says, "Taoism advocates a minimum of . . . intervention, relying instead on individual development to reach a natural harmony." He adds, "Stop trying to control." This organic flow is reflected in free writing, brainstorming, and approaching writers and writing tasks from multiple perspectives. This is not to say that the Tao tosses revision and rigor out the window—as Lao Tzu wrote, "The journey of a thousand miles begins by taking the initial steps" (verse 64). It's simple. We must begin at the beginning.

The great artist and the accomplished athlete begin with small steps and create beauty, complexity, excellence. The writer also must learn in increments, and even the most advanced levels must write in stages. This is what is called the process approach to writing.

The more I explored the connections between the Tao and writing, the more obvious it became that I was on to something. I had read the Tao Te Ching in two versions and would soon read two more, but I was looking for a holistic sense of what it meant to be a Taoist. I had learned that Taoism is not a religion. In fact, the philosophy is so flexible that many people combine Taoism with Christian, Jewish, Moslem, Buddhist, Hindu, and other beliefs (though certain members of these sects would probably argue with those connections). I had a general intellectual understanding of the philosophy, but I wasn't sure I'd know a Taoist when I saw one. That is when I came across a Web site created by Justin Valentin and dedicated to Winnie the Pooh in general and to Benjamin Hoff's book, *The Tao of Pooh*. The site, *www.just-pooh.com*, provides a brief summary of Hoff's book. I had my misgivings at first. Let's face it: a book about the Tao and Winnie the Pooh could be hard to take seriously. After all, we're grown-ups. But when I saw references to this "silly little book" in other articles, I picked up a copy and discovered that it was not so silly after all.

In the book's introduction Hoff describes how in Taoism the wheel is defined by the spaces between the spokes and the bowl by the emptiness within the form. This reminded me of the technique in art of focusing on negative space to create more effective representations of objects. In writing we often forget the importance of the space between structure and the advantages of writing without rules. One experiment conducted with writing students reported that the ones who were stuck in their writing tended to be those who were trying hard to follow the rules they had learned from their teachers. The ones who admitted that they were "doing it all wrong" and who were striving to find their own strategies were more often successful in creating effective text. This is not to say that writers must break the rules of good writing (at least not all the time), but they should know when a rule helps and when it doesn't and, most importantly, they should follow their instincts. The successful writers described above were those who followed the Tao as they used the spokes and the spaces to create the written wheel.

Wu Wei

The recognition of the power of negative spaces relates to an important tenet of the Tao. This concept, Wu Wei, roughly translates to mean "do without doing" (Tao Te Ching, verse 63). When Eeyore loses his tail (as described in *The Tao of Pooh*), the searchers' preoccupation with cleverness, knowing, and business offers little help. Only Pooh, who isn't trying to look, is able to find the tail. This is similar to the way that a writer finds a pearl through brainstorming or free writing—or perhaps more commonly, in relaxing and not thinking about writing. In my own writing experience, this has been true time after time. My dissertation topic came to me in the shower. "Getting Burned," a story I published in *Ellery Queen's Mystery Magazine*, came to me one November evening as my wife and I relaxed before the fireplace. I had been teaching in a local maximum security prison, and one of my students was an infamous arsonist. This odd combination of bits and pieces came together at that moment in front of a gentle fire and allowed a story about an arsonist and an old man to come to me effortlessly.

Another of my published stories emerged from my habit of hiking and camping in the backwoods of northern Michigan where I grew up. I was skirting a ridge, a long rise we called Hogsback Mountain, in a cedar swamp thicket, and I heard what sounded like a mournful keening of something in the distance. I still have no idea what it was—perhaps a bobcat—but as I looked up, I could imagine an even more exotic creature, a Yeti, or Bigfoot, along the ridge above me. This, like much of the best stuff writers do, percolated for several years until it came out as a short story titled "The Keening Woods." The most effective writing teacher often teaches best through a kind of non-action, by allowing student writers the time and space to write.

This is not easy for Westerners. Several years ago when a senior faculty member was scheduling an observation of my advanced composition class, she said, "Make sure you're teaching something when I'm there. Don't just have them writing." The implication, of course, is that nothing is being learned if the teacher isn't the center of action. Clearly, the writing teacher must teach, but most importantly, the writer must have the freedom to write under the teacher's guidance. Of course, it can be difficult to let go of that grip on authority. I recently observed a class being taught by an energetic young composition instructor. She was well prepared and congenial—all in all, a good teacher—and her students had regularly given her glowing evaluations. Even so, the class felt rushed. The instructor asked students to spend a few moments reviewing and commenting on one another's writing. Within a few moments, she had moved on to the next segment of the class. Each time she asked students to spend time writing or thinking about writing, she short-circuited the effort, seemingly unable to allow them the time and space, unable to relinquish control. The Tao opens a space beyond the spokes of the wheel for writing, thinking, and exploring.

Take the Time to Explore

Just as instructors often rush through assignments, beginning writers learn to think quickly, draft quickly, and finish quickly. They learn to write like their instructors—quickly, mechanically, and confusingly, putting words on paper in a haphazard rush that stymies effective writing.

In *The Tao of Pooh*, Benjamin Hoff refers to the episode where Rabbit finds a note left by Christopher Robin that ends "BISY BACKSON" (Christopher meant to say "Busy. Back soon"). Rabbit then spends the rest of the day trying to figure out what a "BISY BACKSON" is.

We might call the rushed situation described above the "Bisy Backson" approach to writing. People following this method confuse exercise with work and activity with creativity. "The Bisy Backson is almost desperately active," says Hoff. He adds, "Let's put it this way: if you want to be healthy, relaxed, and contented, just watch what a Bisy Backson does and then do the opposite" (Hoff, 93).

We are a last-minute culture. Just-in-time production seems to work reasonably well for automobiles and other kinds of manufacturing, but when it becomes a way of life, it makes most

19

of us crazy. I often find myself in the Bisy Backson rut. Let's face it, we writing instructors tend to think we have to be teaching something or we're not doing our jobs. "Teaching something" usually means droning on about comma-splices and thesis statements and seeing how many mistakes we can find in someone's writing. In their book *A Community of Writers*, Zemelman and Daniels tell us that writing does not come through teaching, but through learning. Writers don't become writers because a teacher has lectured on the properties of good writing, on grammar, structure, and all of that. We become writers by experiencing writing, and no amount of Bisy Backson activity will change that. Thus, the teacher who is afraid to open space and time for students to explore through writing, to let them relax and be writers, to let them write, will produce those students who make it clear that they "can't write" and, moreover, "hate writing."

If you want to be a writer, just watch what conventional, linear writers do and then do the opposite, or at least, do something different. While the Bisy Backson writer is madly dashing off a magnificent first and only draft, you should daydream, jot a few words on blue or green paper, talk to friends, gather ideas like stones on a beach. When the Bisy Backson writer is moving on to the next quick paper, write something, begin to put ideas on paper. When the Bisy Backson is feverishly working to fulfill an assignment or writing exercise, to put sentences into a correct form, and to get the punctuation and syntax just right, write for feeling and power and style. And when the Bisy Backson writer is hyperventilating in the hall, waiting for the teacher to post grades, then weeping over the C or B or A-, sit back, have a cup of tea, read a book. Take a walk, write, breathe. Write to enjoy the sensation of the pen rolling across the lines of a legal pad and to savor the beauty of smooth black lines on clean white bond.

Some writers focus too much on the final product before they've begun the journey. In *The House at Pooh Corner*, Pooh considers what he likes best in the world. He decides the "moment just before you begin to eat it [honey] . . . was better than when you were" (Hoff, 110). In effect, it is the journey, or the process, that we should most enjoy.

This, of course, goes against the typical writer's attitude toward a writing task. For a student with a writing assignment, the goal is to get it done, hand it in, and get a good grade—and the only acceptable grade is an A. For other writers, the goal may be to get a story submitted for publication, and the only positive outcome is a glowing acceptance letter. The process itself is seen as punitive, with success or failure entirely determined by someone else's decision.

Pooh would tell these writers to enjoy the process, to see it as an opportunity to create, to develop, and, above all, to understand the central role of change and growth in life. Experienced writers know this and will tell us that a paper, article, book, letter, etc., is never actually finished. Practicality requires that we stop somewhere in the process, but nothing actually says we can't keep on writing and revising. In fact, most writers continue to develop ideas and themes from one book to the next in what is essentially a lifelong evolution and revision.

Some will say that it all sounds very good in theory, but this Wu Wei approach isn't very practical. Students need to fulfill assignments and receive grades, or else they aren't learning. Serious writers are supposed to measure their success by the quantity of their published works. Of course, we know better, but we've always done it the Bisy Backson way. Change is hard.

Part 2

Twelve Principles
of the Tao of Writing

1. Writing is natural:

nature

"Even when he [the sage] travels far, he is not separate from his own true nature."
(Tao Te Ching, verse 25)

"The motion of nature is cyclic and returning."
(verse 40)

The Need to Communicate

Writing is natural, isn't it? Many writers will find this hard to believe. For too many of us, novices and experienced writers alike, writing is an odious, painfully rigid task that offers few rewards. It is anything but natural. Our image of writing tends to come from our school years, and our memory of school writing can be painful. As a result, in school our objective, and the best that could be hoped for, was to finish a writing assignment, hand it in, and survive with a passing grade.

In fact, writing is a natural extension of the human need to communicate. Of course, it is more conscious, and in this way, more complex than speech. We are saddled with the burden of learning to read and write print, with the technology of writing; however, we tend to do it relatively well in spite of the barrage of negative messages we receive as we strive to become writers.

Yes, that's right: Most people are fairly proficient communicators when they reach adulthood. Most can even communicate complex ideas in writing. They may not be able to do it in the "King's English," the cultural standard, but even remedial writers tend to be able to negotiate the written word effectively—in the right context. We don't naturally use language to complete assignments and tasks that are given to us. We use language to communicate.

Writing is natural when we approach it in ways that mine our "own true nature," that allow us to let go of the overt mechanics of writing assignments and just do it. A way to illustrate this is to think about what you've written lately. Let's say you work in a sales department, and you've just written a memo on some problems with recent sales training programs, some paragraphs for the back of a new brochure, and an e-mail to a prospective client. Or maybe you're a student who has recently

27

written an essay on the Yin and Yang of *Hamlet*, a five-page art history paper, and, finally, an essay exam in sociology.

Now let's think about the other writing you do, the natural writing. You may have written an e-mail or even a letter to a friend. You might have penned a poem, or a clever limerick to celebrate someone's birthday or promotion at work. You may have fired off a letter to the editor of the local paper over an issue that concerns you, or a letter of complaint to the manufacturer of a cleaning product that didn't really make your whites whiter and your brights brighter. You may have even written a eulogy for a loved one. Recently after my father experienced a severe stroke and I waited for the news that his life support had been shut off, I wrote him a letter. It was my private conversation, and it turned out that it would become the eulogy at his funeral. This is profound writing, the kind of text that reflects who we are, the kind that comes from deep inside us, emerging naturally with joy, sadness, humor, pride, anger, and frustration.

I'm a songwriter, and throughout the years I've written hundreds of songs. Not all of them are masterpieces, but nearly all are reflections of natural writing. When I look back at this collection of songs, I see that they seem to outline and highlight important parts of my life. "Arizona Flower" came out of a time when I was learning to play the banjo and mandolin and was living in the desert outside of Phoenix; "Darling Comrade" was a product of the year I spent in China; and "Mother Earth" was a song of environmental awareness I wrote during my years in a small town with a big activist tradition. And then, of course, as with almost all songwriters, I have written countless love songs.

This is natural writing. Look back at the personal letters, short stories, poems, songs, journal entries, plays, essays, and more that you may have written over the years. They have emerged from your life, your experiences, relationships, successes and failures, and they flow seamlessly in and out, like colored threads, impossible to separate from the rest of you. We simply need to recognize that writing is natural. Children love to write until we squeeze the wonder and joy, the very purpose out of writing through artificial, punitive, mind-numbing, contrived exercises, drills, and assignments. It doesn't have to be this way. We all have a natural flow in us, an ability, even a desire, to communicate the profound parts of our lives. This is the way.

Natural writing can also rise from our interaction with and the inspiration of the natural world. The powerful, some would say revolutionary, writing of Edward Abbey in *Desert Solitaire* was inspired by the rugged, unforgiving, and beautiful landscape of the Southwest. My own writing students have often produced their best work as the result of a week in the wilderness, a confrontation with a force of nature such as a blizzard or thunderstorm, or—as in the case of one young writer I knew—coming face to face with the creatures of the wild. His particular story was a wonderful narrative of days diving with barracuda and sharks off the Florida Keys.

To say that writing is natural, then, is to acknowledge that writing, at its best, comes from inside, from the most important parts of our lives, from our very nature. At its most fundamental, writing is not right or wrong; it is simply writing. This is not to say that writers can or should be immediately satisfied with "their own voice" in writing, and feel that they should not do anything to change their initial way of expressing themselves. It is also natural to grow in what we do, to become more mature, faster, better in many ways. Writing is no different. It is unnatural to remain static. And, in fact, nothing does.

Take a moment and look at the world around and inside you. Consider the natural elements: the quality of light, the temperature (warm or cold against your skin), and the weather; and consider the textures, plants, colors, and all the qualities of your surroundings. Now think about your inner workings: the flow of blood through your veins, the beating of your heart and rhythm of your breathing. Jot down your observations of the natural inner and outer worlds.

2. Writing is flow:

river

"Nothing on earth is more gentle and yielding than water, yet nothing is stronger. When it confronts a wall of stone, gentleness overcomes hardness; the power of water prevails."
(Tao Te Ching, verse 78)

Writing as the River. Writing as the Wind.

We've often heard sports announcers talking about how an athlete can be "in the zone," a phrase that reflects the athlete's complete absorption in an activity. The intensity of Lance Armstrong in the Tour de France, Mia Hamm in the World Cup of soccer, or Tom Brady in the NFL playoffs is a palpable realization of this zone, of the flow of intensity and creativity. Musicians also often seem to be in something of a trance as they play. We see it in the jazz saxophonist's contortions, the rock guitarist's face, and the violinist's rapture. In her book, *Writing in Flow*, Susan Perry explores this phenomenon, which is referred to as a "state of flow." Some people, it seems, are blessed with a natural tendency to shift into flow almost at will, while others have never felt the stopping of time that characterizes the experience, and some few others live in an almost perpetual state of flow. Artists and craftspeople seem to agree that flow is essential to creativity and productivity. They often describe it as a trance-like experience where they begin working—painting, playing music, carving, building, and such—and they emerge an hour or many hours later with a sense that they have been submerged in some way. Susan Perry writes, "Your sense of self is altered during flow . . . as if you've been participating in some bizarre ritual, as though your body's been taken over by 'something.'" This may seem to be pretty strange stuff—almost mystical, and certainly mysterious. Writing offers that place, that trance-like zone where it seems second nature to improvise and create, and where ideas and text blend in a flowing, ongoing stream.

Experienced writers and teachers talk about coherence, the flow of a text from beginning to end. The essay that reads smoothly is coherent. The writer creates this flow in several ways. First, the invention, or prewriting, stages of the process must be as unencumbered as possible. When a writer first sits down to create text, it is important to *write through*, to write freely and to get words and ideas down without being encumbered by rigid guidelines and rules. This initial flood of words and ideas will come more easily than the novice writer might imagine. But first she has to let go of the expectations, the need to get it right, the need to achieve an impossible ideal. The usual way that we learn to write—rigid assignments, grammar drills, outlines, five paragraph essays, and grades—can be paralyzing to a developing writer; consequently, people tend to lock up when they're faced with writing something. Writer's block is the result of an author's rigor mortis, and it simply does not have to be. Most people have little trouble letting go when they're talking, expounding on a thousand subjects, but when they are asked to write, the flow often stops like a turned-off spigot. It doesn't have to.

Ways to Establish Flow and Coherence

Imagine a brook flowing along quickly over rocks and branches, through small dams of fallen leaves and debris, around tree roots, through metal culverts, and on and on. Then, imagine somebody erecting a brick wall in the brook's path. The forward motion of the stream will stop momentarily, of course, but the flow will not. The water will continue to push against the wall, becoming ever larger—perhaps, as with beaver dams, it may even form a pond behind the wall. The brook's flow has been altered, but it has not been stopped. It will eventually work under, over, around, or through the wall, and its motion will continue. Not only is the wall unable to stop the flow, but it forces the water to take new directions, to expand in ways it could otherwise not have, to find new territory, take new paths.

Now imagine your words are that brook, flowing across a page, over the distance of many pages. The first and last words are separated by that distance, but they are the same water in the same stream. They and all the words in between are part of this continuum, pausing momentarily at the end of each sentence and each paragraph, but flowing all the same.

This flow, the thing that we call coherence, is created in writing in two ways: first, by understanding this interconnection and, second, by learning to use the words and techniques that create a free-flowing narrative or other type of text. Coherence is that smooth flow that carries a reader almost effortlessly from idea to idea, sentence to sentence, page to page, beginning to end. It tends to come naturally to us until we try to do it intentionally in formal writing situations. When we tell a friend a story, we use language that creates a flow in time: *first . . . then . . . after that . . . before . . . next,* and so on. Now and then we go back, reiterate, and remind the listener of our point. And we use a consistent language and a tone that reflects the situation and our intentions. In the very book that you are reading right now, for example, connections are created for each of the listed attributes of Taoist writing simply by numbering them from one to twelve. Further momentum is established with certain words: *next, then, after,* and such. A few important concepts are reiterated when necessary. If this is done successfully, you (the reader) will stay involved and keep moving on through the text.

These and other mechanical devices are essential parts of revising for coherence, but the first part of creating flow is creating text, writing. One of the most effective ways of creating flow right from the start is to get as much on paper as possible before moving on to revising. This sounds like a good idea, but it isn't always easy to get the words down. We hear about writers who sit down and, inspired, create a brilliantly flowing text almost from whole cloth. We may even have experienced this kind of pure writing ourselves in some way. It is a rare thing when creativity, like a spigot, seems to open up and then flow almost instantaneously and unencumbered.

For most of us this is a fantasy. Writing tends to be a more deliberative process, yet a freer flow of words can be developed with practice. The freewrite that is discussed later in the book is, perhaps, the most effective way to open the flow. Another proven and powerful method is to set out a period for writing each day and to do nothing else during that time. I myself like to write around 5:30 or 6 o'clock in the morning when my family is still sleeping, and I try to write briefly before turning in each night. The more regularly you write, the more you'll be able to get a lot written in a free, flowing way. With a lot of practice and using free writing or other methods, your early writing will be substantial and will have a natural flow.

Take a moment right now to write. Pick up your favorite pen, or sit down at the keyboard, and write out your thoughts without worrying about spelling, punctuation, perfect word choice, or even what you're saying. Do this without stopping for ten minutes. When ten minutes have passed read over what you've written. You might be surprised.

3. Writing is creation:

create

"The creative principal unifies the inner and external worlds."
(Tao Te Ching, verse 25)

The Yin and Yang of Creation

Creation is what we do while we're waiting to die, and if we're lucky, we do it pretty well. If we're not, we sit around watching reruns of *I Love Lucy*, eating potato chips, and drinking Diet Coke, or Pepsi, or "lite" beer—and we fall asleep. We don't even know when, finally, out of boredom and frustration, we die. And, even though we will die just the same, we can choose to stay awake, to create. When we create, we live. When we make love, when we lose ourselves in the passion and intense sensation of coupling, our beautiful matter blends creating new matter, new life, and we are alive. When we take sticks and paste and crayons and cobble them together into God knows what, we are alive. When we throw great swathes and blobs of color against barren walls, or sing a lullaby to a child, or knit our first rough scarf, we are alive.

Creation is both the act and the celebration of this magic, the fleeting mystery that is to be alive. Recently, one of my colleagues died suddenly. I knew him at work as a fine teacher and a remarkably pleasant person at 7:30 in the morning—like me he was a morning person. I then learned that he was also a father, a husband, a world-class musician, and the author of numerous books. There is no doubt that he was much more than this and that he created much while he lived. Creation is what we do while we're alive, to be alive. Creation is what we do until we die.

Within each of us is the power and the need to create. Our primal urge is to procreate, to bring life to this world. Beyond that we are also driven, it seems, to build, to embellish, to color—to enrich our environment in countless ways. At the same time, we strive to create and recreate ourselves. We take courses in painting, yoga, auto repair, woodworking, gardening, gourmet cooking, music, and on and on. We are creative by nature. This doesn't change when we begin to write.

We like to think of certain people or types as creative. Vincent van Gogh, Miles Davis, and Willa Cather are examples of creative people who seem bigger than life. In our dualistic world and mindset (Democrat/Republican, educated/uneducated, good/evil, black/white), we may put certain exceptional people on one side of the creativity divide and ourselves on the other. In truth, we are all creative beings. Many of us simply fail to recognize our creative nature, and we define creativity far too narrowly. What's more, we tend to misjudge what it means to be creatively productive, thinking of those rare and wonderful "creative" folks as being blessed with an almost magical gift.

Certainly many artists, the kind of folks we usually identify as creative, are gifted individuals, but so are we all. We fail to recognize just how creative we are in our lives, in the day to day activities that make us human: our activism, teaching, fitness, in the ways we prepare and share food, even in our relationships. Osho, an influential Indian mystic and spiritual leader, says: "Creativity means loving whatsoever you do—enjoying, celebrating it!" (Osho, 93). If you wash dishes in a joyful, loving way, you are creative. In effect, we are creative beings whether or not we ever pick up a paintbrush or sing a song. There is no doubt that we are creative when we put words on paper.

Each time we write, we create a connection between the inner and external worlds we inhabit. The Tao would have us freely explore this sense of newness, of beginning, of communion, and of change.

As in physics, where we recognize that for every action there is an equal and opposite reaction, in the Way, yin is always balanced by yang. We create and we destroy. We build, and we raze. We embellish, and we deface. This eternal cycle is the Tao.

It seems, then, that although the Way bears a great creative force, it is equally destructive.

There is no contradiction here. Creation is not a tidy process. The violence of the erupting volcano results in the apparent death of a landscape. When Mount St. Helens erupted in Oregon in 1980, a northern forest was flattened, its vast greenery replaced by a dead, gray moonscape. People and animals died, and a poisonous black smoke hung in the air, spreading across hundreds of miles. Hawaii, parts of Italy, Japan, Mexico, and other places around the world have experienced similar and even far worse destruction at the feet of the fire mountains.

Of course, we know that out of this devastation comes life. Volcanic ash creates fertile soil, and from that emerges the abundance needed to support a rich variety of life. In the same way, forest fires allow a forest to thrive; floods deposit thick, nutritious silt across depleted farmlands; and the bitter cold and snow of winter is a time of rest and rejuvenation for the land.

Nothing in life, or in art, remains the same forever. One gentle example of impermanence is the sand painting of Tibetan monks; another is the array of beautiful sidewalk chalk creations of street artists in Paris, London, and New York. The ephemeral quality of such works is part of, and even essential to, their beauty. When the wind blows the sand back to its own natural form or the rain washes away the rich colors of sidewalk art, these destructive elements of nature release beauty into the universe and, like a river, it flows on. Children know that their sand castles will collapse into a rising tide or under another child's feet, yet they continue creating their minarets and battlements and, when one castle is washed away, they gleefully begin a new one.

From my own experience, I have been making ornate piñatas for my children's birthdays for most of their lives. These creations of newspaper, flour, and water take many hours and, I've been told, are pretty nifty and unique. When they're broken, piñatas release candy and small prizes, of course, but they also release a sense of wonder and magic. Children often take the idea home and, when their birthdays come around, they too are helping their parents create unique piñatas. When my children grew older, they no longer wanted piñatas, and that saddened me somewhat. Then my daughter said that one day, when she has kids, she assumes grandpa will be making piñatas for their birthdays. I hope so, but I suspect that with or without me, they will carry this small but enduring tradition to their own families and friends. It is like the cycle of creation and destruction that we see in music. A note sounds and is gone. Yet, it endures.

The act of writing is an act of creation. We put words down in passion or joy, in a mood of reverence or anger, in love or despair. We write our diaries and journals, our letters and memos, our short stories and poems, our articles and novels, knowing that, at some level, our words matter. Like a piñata or sand painting, the written word brings meaning into the universe. Some might say we create meaning when we write. And, like the ethereal arts, writing will eventually blow away on a gust of wind. Even the ancient writings of the Dead Sea Scrolls, the Bible, the Koran, and the Tao will fade, but like music, their essence lingers.

When we understand the ethereal nature of our writing, we can accept and celebrate the cycle of creation and destruction in our own writing process. In writing, if we're wise, we learn to let go of our words. We learn to throw out our pet phrases. We cut sections, replace words, revise arguments, and, if we are honest writers, jettison pages, chapters, manuscripts—and we begin again, but each time with the collected wisdom of our greater experience and growth. Writing is messy. We create in the crucible of that chaos. Out of invention and revision, of writing, rejecting and writing again and again, the writer grows. The Tao is creative. There is no difference between birth and death, building and tearing down. It is all part of creation. From this cycle of creation and destruction, the writer evolves. From this revelation, the writer learns to create.

Take a moment to create. Sketch a pencil drawing, arrange a collection of stones, dance a new step, or write a poem.

4. Writing is detachment:

free

"The sage does not try to change the world by force for he knows that force results in force. He avoids extremes and excesses and does not become complacent."
(Tao Te Ching, verse 29)

The Creative Power of the Empty Vessel

To build a house in the world of man
And not to hear the noise of horse and carriage,
How can this be done?
When the mind is detached, the place is quiet.
I gather chrysanthemums under the eastern hedgerow
And silently gaze at the southern mountains.
The mountain air is beautiful in the sunset,
And the birds flocking together return home.
In all these things there is real meaning,
Yet when I want to express it, I become lost in no-words.
—T'ao Ch'ien

For many years, I made the rounds of clubs, hotels, and bars, singing and playing my guitar solo, with a partner, and as part of a five-piece band. From night to night, I had to remember the music, lyrics, and arrangements of more than one hundred songs. It always amazed me that, when I consciously tried to remember the lyrics of songs, I'd stumble, forgetting a few words here, a verse there. On the other hand, when I simply started singing, I would get through the music without error. To this day, I can remember songs I haven't even thought of in twenty-five years if I just begin playing them. I've learned that I can't force this recall but must let it come to me.

Writing is like this. The more we demand that a theme or a story idea come to us, the more likely we are to be faced with writer's block, and the more we try to write well, the more it sounds forced, pompous, stiff. The Taoist writer writes first by opening up to the flow of ideas that come naturally. Unfortunately, most of us have worked hard to keep this flow shut in, to keep our creative natures tightly closed. We need help breaking through this wall. Fortunately, there are ways to untie even the most tightly cinched knot.

The detached writer shuts off the critic inside and is freed from the constraints of rules and structure, at least in the early stages of the writing project. An effective way of showing the critic the door is through free writing. When novice writers first encounter the freedom of free writing, many choke. They find it almost painful to write without correcting, editing, outlining, scratching out—without monitoring their text for errors. It seems to bring on something akin to an anxiety attack in many people. They've never been asked to write freely and don't quite know how to go about it, how to shut off the self-censoring mechanism that has been part of writing for their entire lives. Once they break through that self-imposed wall, however, the words begin to flow, unattached to the chains of structure and restrictive rules.

The Magic of Free Writing

Free writing is as close to magic as anything you are likely to experience in writing. It can give you story ideas, article topics, and more; through it, you may be able to break through writing logjams by appealing to your inner voice.

Free writing works by releasing the inhibitions we associate with having to write a certain form in a certain way. It literally frees writers to produce text. There is no mystery to its effectiveness. First, it's very simple—almost too simple for people like ourselves, who have been raised in a culture that seems to grow more and more complicated every day. We're suspicious of simplicity. Free writing is unconstrained by the need to be neat, the obsession to be right, or the fear that our writing will not be grammatically correct. Once novice writers grasp the significance of this, their writing begins to flow. Writers who find it virtually impossible to write for three or four minutes at the outset are often surprised to find themselves writing for fifteen, twenty, twenty-five minutes, or longer, without realizing it, and wanting to go on. We all have an inner voice, often an intimate understanding of the uses and structure of language, one that can translate to the written page fairly easily if we are able to let the words flow. Free writing helps us do this.

Free writing is a key to the doorway into "the zone." It bypasses those rigid barriers we have constructed over many years. The barriers are tall, wide, and difficult to surmount, but the Tao simply flows through the cracks, over and around in its own, gentle way, and the barriers no longer bar the writer's voice.

Free writing is the manifestation of the Tao, and it is no wonder that it is as difficult as it is for Western writers, the Bisy Backsons of the world. We're told from the start that we must be correct. Our sentences have to be complete, our spelling must be perfect, and our grammar must be exact. In effect, we are constrained by our need to be perfect, a most unfortunate obsession. It is a disease of our culture that affects us in more than our writing. We struggle to be petite, to have the physique of an eighteen-year-old athlete, to have flawless skin, the perfect tan and sparkling white teeth, to have a high enough IQ to qualify for Mensa, to have the most prestige, make the most money, drive the fastest car—in effect, to be something that simply doesn't exist in the real world. The key term here is "struggle." The Tao tells us that to struggle is to create barriers, and to do this is to be the cause of our own difficulties.

Remember the lesson of the river. It flows around impediments effortlessly. This is the law of Wu Wei, to do without doing. Free writing allows us to write without writing as we have learned it has to be done. The constraints are gone. The result is that words and ideas are free to flow unencumbered by preconceptions or the rigid expectations we Bisy Backsons have internalized. It's an amazing thing—almost like magic.

Here is how free writing works. You sit, stand, or lie in a comfortable writing position and open a notepad, word processing screen, napkin, or paper bag. You begin to write. It is important that you simply keep writing, moving the pen or typing without concern for content or correctness—sentence structure, grammar, and spelling. The only rule is that you must keep the words flowing. You say that you can't think of anything to write? Begin by writing "I can't think of anything to write because . . ." and, miraculously, the words will begin to flow.

Beginning writers—indeed, most writers—are intimidated by numbers of words and pages. They look at an article or book and assume they couldn't possibly write so much. Free writing breaks through that barrier. In fact, you will probably find that you can write pages and pages of prose. Just last week in the writing class I teach, I asked a group of writers after a ten-minute free write to check the word count on their computers. Every one of them had written from 350 to 550 words in that short time. Of course, as you will no doubt also find, free writing is often rambling, wandering prose, and a lot of words do not great writing make. Inevitably, though, within your pages of free writing you will find that you have written something special.

Free writing works to help the writer find detachment. The rhythm is natural and creative, and the results are unexpected precisely because the free writer is able to let go of the usual writer's constraints. As soon as the focus becomes spelling or punctuation, the flow is interrupted, the spell broken.

It is not true that free writing, this magically liberating exercise in detachment, is always chaotic. The paradox of Wu Wei is the remarkable productivity of this consciously detached exercise. Even though the very word "product" seems to contradict the spirit of the Tao, this contradiction is as much a part of the way as the river. Free writing mirrors this marvelous paradox in that it can lead to an extraordinary improvement in a writer's ability to write well. Peter Elbow contrasts ordinary writing with free writing in this way: Writing normally "feels like trying to steer, to hold things together, to juggle balls. When I free write, I let go, stop steering, drop the balls and allow things to come to me" (Belanoff et al., 207). This is the detachment of Wu Wei, the doing by not doing. As Elbow also tells us, "Free writing is an invitation to stop writing and instead to be written" (209).

Detachment through Journaling

A journal can be the vehicle for many forms of writing such as free writing, a personal diary, writing and sketching combined, planning, recording observations, drafting more formal writing, creating poetry, and so on. Journaling to achieve detachment is most often a kind of free writing. The detached journal is a comfortable place in which a writer can take chances, can explore without worrying about being judged or criticized. The key, as with many writing techniques, is to enter this place regularly, daily if possible. It's an easy, cheap, and powerful means to better writing. Here are a few simple tips to help the journal writer:

- Find a journal/notebook that you like. Personally, I like the black and white composition books. You may prefer something more formal, perhaps a covered book or a stenographer's tablet. You should enjoy writing in your journal.
- Use a pen that you like because your words are important, and the act of writing should offer you pleasure. I write with a fountain pen my wife gave me, or a smooth roller ball. I like the look and feel of laying down smooth lines of dark black ink.
- Keep the journal with you. If it's not there, you can't write in it.
- Write every day. 'Nuff said.

The Mysterious Detachment of Dreaming

The great Taoist master Chuang Tzu tells a story of the power of dreams:

Chuang Chou dreamed he was a butterfly fluttering among the trees, doing as he pleased, completely unaware of a Chuang Chou. A sudden awakening, and there, looking a little out of sorts, was Chuang Chou. Now, I don't know whether it is Chou who's dreamed he was a butterfly, or whether a butterfly dreams he's Chuang Chou (Chuang Tzu, 18).

Dreams come to us effortlessly, uninvited, unexpected. They are often unwanted, sometimes comforting, or even dazzling. They are rivulets in the flow of our lives. In dreams we find inspiration, terror, seduction, confusion, and enlightenment—the gamut of human experience. Dreams are a special part of each of us and of our unconscious mind; they spring from our deepest nature, sneaking up on us when our guard is down.

Most of us have heard stories about writers, musicians, and painters—artists of all kinds—whose dreams are so compelling that they inspire or even forecast in whole the artist's work.

Such powerful dreams, even when uninvited, can inspire our work and bring us closer to ourselves, but dreams are often just fleeting collections of images and motion. They don't last or have much to say to us. That is, unless we pay close attention. Dream researchers tell us we can remember our dreams in detail. They suggest that, to do this, you keep a pen and pad near your bed. Then, as soon as you wake from a dream, you can write down the fresh experience. The more you do this, the more you are apt to remember your nocturnal voyages. These dream journal entries can help you to tap into the creative source that each of us has. Many may inspire you right then to jot down stories, essays, or ideas for projects. More often they'll lay quiet for a time and emerge later in free writes and journal entries, or even stories or songs.

We also have the ability to invite dreams. These include lucid dreams, daydreams, and meditations. The dreamer learns to tap into the Tao by letting go of control and allowing the stream to flow over and through, bringing with it what we sometimes call inspiration.

Lucid dreaming is a technique for consciously using dreams to help yourself find a solution or to experience something not possible in the waking world. When practicing lucid dreaming, you learn to ask for certain dreams and then control your experiences while dreaming. Lucid dreaming can be a powerfully creative tool, though it is beyond the scope of our discussion here. If you would like to learn more about lucid dreaming, you can explore some of the many good books, Web sites, and advisors on this topic.

To Dream, Perchance to Write

We all daydream. It gets us through a long commute, and it takes our minds off of a droning presenter (though it may have gotten our ears boxed by Sister Mary Joseph in elementary school). Daydreams, like their nighttime counterparts, are a letting go of time and place. They can offer a pleasant respite from enforced focus and can be a rejuvenating part of a long day. They can bring us insight—the "aha!" moment, allowing us to let go, to stop trying so hard. Marion Milner writes, "In daydreaming, there is no action, thought is just playing with itself . . . mind and body meeting in expressive action" (Milner, 74). In that moment of Wu Wei, of not doing, we can discover our creative selves.

From my own writing experience, I can remember sitting in front of a blazing fireplace one winter evening. I was half dozing, daydreaming, when the idea came to me for my short story titled (appropriately enough) "Getting Burned." Mihaly Csikszentmihalyi suggests that we are often the most creative in these moments of seeming inattention. He describes the "aha" moments of prominent people in business, science, and the arts, profound moments that just seemed to happen while these people were engaged in essentially meditative activities, whether it is strolling down a path, jogging, driving, or fishing. It seems that creative people often find the elusive "moment of insight" during these times of unawareness in what Marion Milner calls a "fertilizing" quality. This powerful gift of daydreaming is open to all of us and is a kind of meditation.

The Wakeful Detachment of Meditation

Often seen as a "controlled dream" of sorts, meditation is perhaps the most powerful and proactive of all the processes described in this section. When we meditate we allow our minds to move to a place of deep relaxation where we are able to explore either in a guided manner or to allow the subconscious mind to delve into its creative corners in a free, open way. As a writer, you can utilize the power of meditation in several ways.

Meditation for Preparation

You may meditate to prepare for writing—clearing the mind, easing the body's tensions, and letting go of the day's flotsam. Relaxation and breathing meditation can act as a bridge between the troubled, troubling world and your writing.

Perhaps the simplest form of meditation you can do is a basic breathing meditation. It can be done in many ways. Take a moment to experience this easy, effective breathing mediation:

A simple breathing meditation

The first stage of meditation is to stop distractions and make your mind clearer and more lucid. This can be accomplished by practicing this simple breathing meditation.

1. Choose a quiet place to meditate and sit in a comfortable position. You can sit in the traditional cross-legged posture or in any other position that is comfortable. If you wish, you can sit in a chair. The most important thing is to keep your back straight to prevent your mind from becoming sluggish or sleepy.
2. Sit with your eyes partially closed, what Tibetan Buddhists call "soft eyes." Focus your gaze gently on

something in front of you, and turn your attention to your breathing. Breathe naturally, preferably through the nostrils, without attempting to control your breath, and try to become aware of the sensation of the breath as it enters and leaves the nostrils. This sensation is your object of meditation. Try to concentrate on it to the exclusion of everything else.

At first, your mind will be very busy, and you might even feel that the meditation is making your mind busier; but in reality you are just becoming more aware of how busy your mind normally is.

There will be a great temptation to follow the different thoughts as they arise, but resist this. Remain focused to the exclusion of everything else on the sensation of the breath. If you discover that your mind has wandered and is following your thoughts, immediately return it to the breath. Repeat this as many times as necessary until the mind settles on the breath.

Meditation for Inspiration

As a writer, you can also meditate to explore internal places and ideas. Guided meditation and visualization can allow you to create worlds, characters, and situations and to "try them on" before committing words to paper.

A simple guided meditation

Before beginning this meditation, a few words on relaxation:

You should be sitting or lying comfortably. Sitting tends to be best because meditating is so relaxing that it's also a great way to fall asleep on one of those tense evenings.

Relax. This is easier said than done, but here are three simple methods that may work to relax you. One method is to focus and slowly count breaths to ten, following the breathing meditation described in the last section. A second way of relaxation that works its magic simply and quickly is the staircase. Close your eyes and imagine a staircase going down ten steps before you. With each step down tell yourself you are becoming more and more relaxed until, upon reaching the last step, you are completely relaxed. A third relaxation method that is commonly used is to tense and relax muscle groups, one after another, beginning with your feet, moving to your calves, thighs, and buttocks, and then to your stomach, hands, arms, shoulders, neck, and face.

All right then, now that you feel completely relaxed, we can begin.

Imagine a wonderful place. It's up to you. You decide what is wonderful. It can be a safe place, a place of great beauty. You can also experiment with other kinds of places. Instead of the usual safe, warm, beautiful place, you might visualize a place of excitement, even danger and suspense if that gets your blood flowing.

See the place in detail—the light, the colors, the textures. Move through it, and take in every aspect of the surroundings. What do you see? What are the sensations, the sounds, the scents? Immerse yourself and your senses fully in this world. Add to the scenery, manipulate the environment in any way you wish. Build paths, buildings, plants. Wander around and become familiar with your place. Create anything you wish. Then populate this new world with people, animals—creatures of any kind. You are limited only by your imagination. When you have explored to your heart's content, return to conscious awareness, and write about the experience in as much detail as you can.

Perspiration

Writing itself can be meditative. We don't meditate to become good meditators—we meditate to get in touch with ourselves, to be at peace with the greater universe, to be fully in the moment. We meditate to relax and to soften the edges of the world. Writing meditation is not meant to create great writing, although it may help us to do so. It allows us to be in the moment. The flow of ink on paper, the movement of mind and pen, and our ability to lose ourselves in the very act of writing combine in a powerful, creative way of meditation.

A writing meditation

Take a few moments to relax. Sit comfortably with pen and paper on a table, clipboard, or in a notebook in front of you. If you are very comfortable with a computer keyboard, you might choose to write electronically. In any case, be sure to use writing tools you like. Now close your eyes partially, softly, so you are focusing on nothing in particular. Begin to breathe slowly, consciously. Bring your awareness to your breathing. Silently say I am breathing in; I am breathing out. Do this until you feel calm and centered.

Now pick up your pen and begin to write. Write slowly, in smooth lines. Do not force a topic. Do not write for correctness. Write to write.

Put the pen down, relax your body, and bring your awareness back to your breathing. Breathe consciously for a few more minutes. You may want to read what you have written and to use this creative output for more writing, drawing, musical composition, or whatever you wish. On the other hand, you may want to put the writing meditation away to go back to at a later time, or you may choose to discard it as an ephemeral experience of the moment.

Do this for ten minutes at first. After a number of days and weeks, you may write for far longer.

Take a moment to let go. Find a quiet place where you, a pad of paper, and your pen can detach from the world. Begin writing down your worries and concerns. This can be in a list, as a free write, a poem, or any form you wish. It's up to you. When you've written everything down, look at it, and destroy it. Tear it up, toss it away, burn it (carefully), just get rid of it. Then begin writing again. This time write down your joys and strengths.

5. Writing is discovery:

discover

"The Tao may be known and observed without the need of travel; the way of the heavens might be well seen without looking through a window.
The further one travels, the less one knows.
So, without looking, the sage sees all, and by working without self-advancing thought, he discovers the wholeness of the Tao."
(Tao Te Ching, verse 47)

Surprise!

As a writer, when you begin to create in a detached, flowing way, the writing is a source of discovery. All creative writers, poets, keepers of bedroom journals, and paper bag lyricists know this. Introspective explorations of love, love lost, teenage angst, difficult decisions, dreams, disappointments, and on and on are the writing workshops of discovery. This even holds true at a highly organized level. Corporate boards, political think tanks, and committees of all kinds brainstorm, cluster, list, and free write to generate ideas, find solutions, and discover.

To deny discovery is to impose a dull sameness on the world, to ignore the reality that the world and the people in it are always new. The universe is rich with the wealth of discovery. When we try to paint a monotone gray over life, we pull a thick blanket over the surprises. Then they lay too long in wait, collecting in their dark places under the surface until, devoid of light and air, they no longer resemble surprises but begin to mutate, to become the monsters in the shadows. Writing is a place to seek out and turn such monsters into wonderful, if not always cheerful, surprises.

These may be as delightful as finding the most beautifully painted egg on Easter morning is for a child. Do you remember how you felt when you first discovered a secret place, a flower, or a new book? Surprises may be rewarding in many ways: discovering a brother you didn't know you had (as I did some years ago); winning a basket of special goodies or even winning the lottery; receiving flowers, or growing a new flower; or learning something new and exciting about an old friend or acquaintance. On the other hand, surprises may be troubling or terrifying: perhaps learning something unpleasant about our own or someone else's nature that contradicts our impression of that person, hearing about a disaster, losing a loved one, or meeting any number of unfortunate or confusing circumstances.

When we embark on the quest that writing is, we acknowledge the unpredictable, the Tao, and open ourselves to the endless potential of discovery.

It isn't easy, this quest. Children grow and develop partly through a process of discovery. When babies explore their small world, they gradually enlarge their actual physical environment and their realm of experience. Every time a child tries something new, chances are, her zone of comfort expands as well. Yet, there always remains that space just beyond reach; as the child reaches or is guided into this new territory, he grows. An eighth-grade English teacher once told me that she loved teaching writing to kids because, "When they start writing, things come out of their heads that are just incredible." Her students themselves were often surprised and delighted by what they discovered and created through writing. Adults are not so different. We can expand our comfort zone when we go away to college, take a new job, move to another state, travel abroad, try a new food, or get on stage at an open mic, and we also discover new spaces through writing.

At the most concrete level, discovery in writing is the process of finding a topic and something to write about it. We all know the feeling of staring at a blank page, sometimes with a deadline looming over us. Classes in English and in writing teach a number of ways to break through the wall of writer's block and to develop a topic; these include free writing, mapping and clustering, listing, brainstorming, and research. In this book, a number of variations on these strategies are discussed and explained. For now, let's move beyond such techniques to try to reach an understanding of the deeper meaning of discovery itself.

Lao Tzu tells us, "The way of the heavens might be well seen without looking through a window." We need not fly to the moon to discover its mysteries or wonders, and we need not have a cup of coffee with a god to understand what it is to be godly. The universe, the Tao, is inside each of us waiting to be discovered.

Writing is, essentially, an act of discovery. There are two important ways in which we discover while we write. We discover what we will say in the writing of it. Again, there is that marvelous contradiction that plays out in so many writing sessions as we forge theories, questions, answers, and more questions. And, through writing, we can discover ourselves.

What We Don't Know, We Can Write

One of the wonderful surprises in writing is that it rarely means just putting what you know down on paper. Fiction writers often find their stories in the act of writing them. Characters grow and behave according to who they are. Many writers will say they rarely know what a character will do until it is written.

In contrast, many beginning writers will try to create characters they know all too well. There are no surprises here. The most dramatic example of this, and certainly one of the most common, is the main character who is a version of the author. Now we all learn to write about what we know, and just about every character you might write has a bit of yourself in him or her. But they are not you. When a writer relates too closely with his or her character, problems are inevitable. First, most of us aren't willing to go out on a limb to be outrageous, controversial, or even painfully honest with our own persona. Rarely does a writer create an autobiographical character who does something horrible, embarrassing, or morally repugnant. We're just

65

too careful with our egos. On top of that, we think, "What if Mom, or Dad, or Aunt Millie saw this?"

Secondly, a character modeled after the writer tends to be shallow. As soon as we decide, consciously or not, that a character is a version of us, acting like us and sharing our boundaries, we fence the character in, and it becomes virtually impossible to let the story and conflict create and discover who the character might be. And, sadly, the character that comes directly from us tends to be boring. No offense, but most of us are not the stuff of fiction. Even the most exciting lives are exciting in brief moments, while the rest of the time is spent eating, going to the bathroom, working, watching television, jogging, reading, and on and on—all respectable activities of normal lives, but not very interesting. A story is an extraordinary moment of conflict and struggle, and we find those moments through discovery and surprise. "The further one travels, the less one knows," says the Tao. Discovery is that journey into the unknown.

It's hardly surprising that we can discover unknown worlds and people in writing fiction. After all, fiction is pretend, a wonderful lie that can illuminate truth. What may be surprising, however, is just how important a role discovery plays in less imaginative kinds of writing.

Discovering New Worlds

Writing has had a powerful influence on the development of modern civilization. In oral cultures, stories and traditions are passed along from person to person, and though these cultural tales may change over time, they tend to remain limited by the limitations of our human brains and memories. Writing is different. It allows us to create a story, a recipe for food or medicine, a scientific theory, or sociological or political philosophy, and instead of passing that bit of knowledge on from generation to generation by rote, we are able learn from, revise, and build upon that foundation. Each time a writer puts her thoughts about democracy, training the family dog, home brewing, or horticulture into writing, there is the potential for discovery.

We think of Isaac Newton discovering the theory of gravity as almost a cartoon in which Newton is sitting under a tree, dozing, when an apple drops and hits him on the head. He then experiences his famous AHA! moment. Newton may not have discovered the properties of gravity specifically through writing, but his notes suggest that he followed a far more systematic scientific process, and writing was at its center. Newton worked through problems in writing, raising questions, analyzing experience, rejecting ideas that did not prove out in his written musings, until he arrived at a conclusion. A moment of inspiration may have led Newton to begin writing, but it was the process of writing that resulted in his enduring, universally known discovery.

Richard Feynman, the brilliant American physicist who is known for his simple, elegant demonstration of the reasons the O-rings failed in the 1983 Shuttle Challenger explosion, claimed to do his scientific work in writing. "You have to work on paper," said Feynman (Gleick, 409). These and many other examples tell us that writing is, in fact, a significant part of discovery in the sciences. We also know that writing is an aspect of discovery in many realms of knowledge that affect our lives: politics, philosophy, medicine, education—the list goes on and on. I write to discover in my own work, and I ask my students to do the same.

Discovery through writing is not just for the great minds of the ages, though. In 1988, Ken Macrorie published a book entitled *The I-Search Paper*. A few years ago, a friend introduced me to this concept. The I-search is a way to explore on paper and to discover first what the writer knows and doesn't know about a subject, then to find answers to important questions and, of course, to discover new questions. Since the publication of Macrorie's book, many middle school and high school teachers have assigned variations of this type of paper to their students. For many of these students, an I-search paper was the first writing they had done that truly excited and engaged them.

The wonderful thing about the I-search approach is that it allows the writer to tell a story in his or her own voice, the story of a search for something important to the writer. My students who create one often tell me they've never written anything like it before, and they enjoy writing, sometimes for the first time. The I-search is a narrative about something important in which the writer explores what she knows, doesn't know, wants to know about a subject. The writer narrates the search, the investigation of sources, the hits and misses, and then goes on to talk (on paper) about her findings. The ending includes a discussion of remaining questions and new directions. The I-search paper is a fresh and personal means of discovering information that is as substantive and important as any formal research paper. Young writers just seem to feel better about it and enjoy it a lot more. The result is good and interesting writing. This book, in fact, started out as an I-search paper.

I don't want to give the impression that the I-search paper is the property of school assignments. In some ways, it illustrates many sides of the Tao. It is a natural way to write, explore, and discover. The writer hunts for answers to questions in the way a child plays hide and seek or hunts for Easter eggs. The hunt results in false starts, wrong turns, and successes. The narrative is a telling of the story of the hunt just as we tell the story of our weekend or vacation to our friends or family. It can be formal, addressing academic or business topics, but it can also help us discover more about ourselves, hobbies, religion—anything that catches our fancy.

The I-search follows a simply, intuitive format that invites the writer in and carries her along. It goes like this:

Find something you want to know more about and write out what it is and why it interests you. Then describe everything you know about it. For example, if you are writing to learn more about fly-fishing in your area and have tried it once or have a friend who has talked about the sport, jot down everything that comes to mind about it. Don't worry about being exact or detailed.

Next, write out what you feel you don't know and want to know about the subject. The act of identifying questions will give you momentum as you begin your search.

In the *Hunt* section, you narrate the experience of looking for information. This can include Internet searches, talking to people to find out what they know, reading and researching in conventional ways, watching video presentations, or even taking a class or workshop. Here, in your own, natural voice—and always in the first-person "I"—you tell the story of the ups and downs of the search.

The *Results* section is where you talk about what you discovered through your search. The novice fly-fisher may have learned something about lures, techniques, equipment, and local streams. Another writer may find out that owning a python is more work and less rewarding than he imagined. The outdoorswoman may locate hiking and climbing resources and be on her way to discovering the great trails of America.

The final part of the I-search lets the writer ask more questions and suggest new directions for exploration and discovery.

I encourage writers to begin writing freely and to resist the temptation to write a "research paper." No question or avenue of discovery is off-base. The direction and flow of the hunt is driven by the writer's interest and curiosity. As the writer tells the story of the search, new questions create excitement, new discoveries create new questions, and the momentum builds. In the end, the writer has often learned and experienced much and is eager to ask, write, and discover more.

Writing as Self-Discovery

Children's author Juanita Havill, in an interview with Anna Olswanger, said, "Writing is an act of discovery, discovering what haunts you, what you need to return to in your life, what you want to say." Writing allows us not only to explore and discover the world around us in its countless manifestations, but it can show us paths to our inner worlds as well—as mentioned above, "the ways of the heavens might well be seen without looking through a window." Writers explore their inner worlds in various ways. Novelists, in creating the fantastic landscapes of science fiction or the dark terrifying passages of a horror story, are tapping into hidden parts of themselves. Therapists use the power of writing to help patients deal with trauma or emotional concerns; psychics use a practice called automatic writing in which the writer is said to be channeling the words of a spiritual entity; and many people write to relax, as a kind of meditation. In all these is a way to self-discovery.

Perhaps the most common window to self-discovery is the journal. Lori Batcheller, a therapist and author, uses journaling extensively in her work. In an article titled "Journal Keeping: A Place for Healing, Self-Discovery, and Creative Flow," she writes, "A journal can be far more than a place to record daily events or idle thoughts. Used purposefully, it can be a catalyst for personal growth, problem solving, and a path to creativity." The key to self-discovery through journaling is in the doing of it, the writing. In an age of complexity, this seems too simple. It *is* simple. First, it's terribly important to spend a few minutes each day writing in a journal. This is not a diary, a day-to-day chronicle. No, it is a space where the writer explores, dreams, and takes risks. Batcheller says, "A journal allows you self-expression without external judgment. It is the perfect tool for clarifying goals and organizing your work day." It's also a way to work through emotional pain and stress, or to come to terms with difficult people, events, and situations. It is no surprise that adolescents spill so much of their emotions onto the pages of diaries and journals. After all, this is the time in our lives of most intense discovery. It is as a teenager that we discover our bodies, many of our desires, our potent emotions, and our voices. Isn't it natural then, and isn't it wonderful that so many teenagers use writing to help them in that time of discovery? Fortunately, you don't have to be sixteen to tap into the power of writing to explore and develop your inner self.

There are no hard and fast rules, but here are a few suggestions for using writing for self-discovery:

• *Find a writing place that is comfortable and feels physically and emotionally safe.* Do you remember, as a teenager, closing your bedroom door and writing? You may have been penning entries in your diary, poems, songs, stories, or letters as you lay sprawled out on your bed. That was your own place then. Mine now is the kitchen table, looking out on our wooded yard, especially in the very early morning hours. It's a quiet, almost meditative place, and I write there more easily than any other place I know.

• *Find a time to write when you won't be disturbed by the kids, your spouse, a roommate, or any other regular distraction.* You may even choose to take the telephone off the hook or turn the ringer off for a brief time. I write best in the early morning, well before my family is out of bed. In fact, this book was created almost entirely before eight o'clock in the morning.

• *Be sure the time you choose is for writing only.* Don't let yourself get distracted by the dirty dishes, the cat, yesterday's newspaper, the radio, or anything else. This is writing time.

• *Commit yourself to writing for a certain amount of time every day.* It doesn't matter whether it's ten, twenty, or sixty minutes. Give yourself time to get the flow moving. Give yourself permission to enjoy the luxury of just writing.

• *Relax before you begin.* Any routine that works for you is fine. You may stretch, meditate, or simply make a cup of tea and lay out your pen and paper. For some people, the simple act of putting pen to paper and letting it take them where it may, is itself relaxation.

• *If getting started is difficult, you can focus your writer's mind on an important question or concern.* A clear lead-in can help. If you are having problems at work, you might begin with something like this: *My job hasn't been very satisfying lately . . .* , or *People at work aren't getting along . . .* Then, simply keep writing. You may ask questions, explore alternatives, create fantasy solutions, or think on paper about your relationship to the problems. Other lead-in phrases can have to do with aspirations or values, and such: *The thing I value most is . . .; Happiness is . . .; The best things about me are . . .; My dreams for the future are . . .; What's bothering me most is . . .*

- *Ask questions.* Try to work through to the answers. Don't worry about being wrong or off-the-wall. The most outrageous answers to the silliest questions can offer insight. Then, from the discussion (your writing), discover new questions.

- *Write about nothing in particular.* Some of our greatest insights come to us in unguarded moments when we have no topic, no agenda. In the spirit of Wu Wei, we often accomplish the most when we do the least.

- *Finally, don't be afraid.* Many of us are afraid to write about what we really feel or believe for fear of offending somebody or, more often, for fear of showing others just how human they are. The fictional character who is not both good and bad, who does not hold embarrassing or unpleasant secrets and desires, is not fully human. As we write for self-discovery, we may discover (or uncover) bits of ourselves that we'd rather leave buried. Remember two things: Only in bringing these hidden artifacts into full sunlight can we see them clearly and deal with them; and, rarely are our deepest secrets and desires unusual, deviant, or extraordinary. They are ultimately what make us human.

Making Sense

When we write, we explore our inner spaces and, in doing so, we soar beyond ourselves, even into the infinite universe. Self-reflection is not always easy, but the rewards are wonderful. Georg Buehler, author of "Seekers Wanted, Apply Within: Finding a Livelihood for the Modern Spiritual Life," writes, "The process of writing can be a powerful tool for self-discovery. It forces the writer to become a student of human nature, to pay attention to his experience, to understand the nature of experience itself. Through delving into raw experience and distilling it into a work of art, the writer is engaging in the heart and soul of philosophy—making sense out of life." Ultimately, when we write, we discover, and discovery leads to change.

Take a moment and look around you. Discover something you hadn't noticed before: that spider in the corner, the way light plays on your ring, a tree in the distance that you've never noticed before. Now write about this discovery.

6. Writing is change:

change

"Through his experience,
The sage becomes aware that all things change."
(Tao Te Ching, verse 2)

Transformations

Chuang Tzu tells us:

Nothing is static. There is no end or beginning to the Tao. Things indeed die and are born, not reaching a perfect state which can be relied on. Now there is emptiness, and now fullness—they do not continue in one form. The years cannot be reproduced; time cannot be arrested. Decay and growth, fullness and emptiness, when they end, begin again. It is thus that we describe the method of great righteousness and discourse about the principle pervading all things. The life of things is like the hurrying and galloping along of a horse. With every movement there is change; with every moment there is alteration. What should you be doing? What should you not be doing? You have only to be allowing this course of natural transformation to be going on. (Chuang Tzu, verse 45)

Beginning writers seem to believe that great writing emerges fully formed from the author's pen. Of course, nothing could be further from the truth. Great writing is created in revision—rethinking, rewriting, adding, subtracting, repositioning, editing. In effect, fine writing is born in change.

We are compelled to change. We change our hair, our style of dress, our way of talking, our friends, our living places, our minds. The world changes. Look around. Much of what you see could not have existed thirty, forty, fifty years ago. Our homes are girded in aluminum and vinyl siding and latex paint. Inside we have computers, microwave ovens, satellite and digital televisions, and telephones that link us through fiber-optic lines.

Writing, too, has changed overtly through the Internet, hypertext, e-mail, and instantaneous online chat rooms. This is the high-tech, public, glitzy face of change some people call progress, but it is not the most profound change occurring in our writing. We write to communicate and to connect with others, and it matters little if we do so on newsprint, twenty-four-pound cotton bond paper, or in pixels on a computer screen. The most significant change you will encounter in writing is not found in the medium or method you use; it is within your writing itself. No matter what instrument you use to write—pen, keyboard, or something yet to be invented—change takes place from the moment we begin to compose. As we jot down ideas, they shift and grow, spawning new ideas. As we start setting these ideas down in written form, the effect is something like the stop-motion nature film footage you may have seen of clouds growing and changing. These films often begin with small, unobtrusive puffs of cloud in an otherwise clear sky. Then, in a process that seems almost seething, the clouds begin to billow and roll, growing like the smoke from Aladdin's lamp, until they have become towering masses of cumulus clouds. Throughout the process, the clouds continue to change from the back forward.

Writing is recursive in this way. As we write, we change what we write. We go back and forth, changing words and sentences, moving paragraphs, adding, cutting, rewording. Many writers even change the beginning of a piece after they've completed the ending. This makes sense, but we tend not to think in these terms, where the ending comes before the beginning, and the middle pops in and out throughout the whole confusing job. That's because it's a messy thing, growing a cloud—or a piece of writing.

As a writer, you should look upon the act of revising not as unavoidable drudgery, but instead as a blessing, a luxury. Writers sometimes tend to think of their work in terms of the Three Fs: fix, finish, and forget. Most people look at revision as "fixing" mistakes. For them revising is not a luxury; it's a pain. But when you believe in what you are writing, when you're interested and invested in the words you put down, and when you have the time and space to write, think, and write some more, revision is no longer punitive.

When Not to Revise

One day recently a writing student of mine asked if I would be willing to read her friend's essay on Post Traumatic Stress Syndrome (PTSS). This student's friend had served in the Vietnam conflict and has experienced firsthand the horrors of that war. Now, suffering from severe and debilitating PTSS, he had taken to writing. I said I would be happy to read the piece, but I would not evaluate it. I just don't believe that all writing should be critiqued. In fact, most writing serves its purpose merely in its being written. It turns out that the writing was excellent—powerful, important, and, as it happens, structurally and grammatically strong. I learned a lot about PTSS, and after the first few lines I was hooked; the piece drew me along almost effortlessly.

Because I knew that the writer was hoping to publish the piece somewhere, and he had asked for my advice, I told my friend to pass along a few critical comments. If the writer had not asked for my critical opinion about whether the writing was good, or if it had been completely uninteresting, disorganized, rife with error, and, in general, poorly written, I would have taken what the writer offered and said "thank you" without critiquing the piece. But in any case, I suspect I would have learned something important, and the writer would have written something important.

We need to recognize that writers should not revise everything, and it isn't the reader's job to critique and correct every word a writer creates. In the case of the Vietnam vet, the writing was both therapeutic and artful. When we free write, or journal, or when we simply want to write in the moment, revising would be pointless, and in most cases, counterproductive. Writing can be an end in itself, and the power of change is inherent in creating something new and fresh. Chuang Tzu tells us that change happens and encourages us to open ourselves to it. For many kinds of writing, however, we release the soul of our text when we revise. Still, this does not mean that the writing ends there. Change is inevitable.

Seeing for the First Time Through "Seeing Again"

Writing is evolutionary. Even the Vietnam vet who writes an essay and leaves it in a journal will probably write another essay. Each new essay contains a piece of past work and, by virtue of this evolutionary process, is part of a much deeper change than we find with simple revision. Yet revision is an immediate expression of change, of our consciously allowing "this course of natural transformation to be going on" (Chuang Tzu, verse 45).

Revision literally means "to see again." When we return to something we've written, we are invited to see it with fresh eyes, to read as a reader rather than as an author. We all know how difficult that can be. Here are ways to overcome that difficulty:

Give your writing the benefit of time and space. Let it lie for a day, two, or even better, a week or more. When you return to it, chances are you'll see it from a fresh, relatively unfamiliar angle. During your absence your mind will continue to ponder the work, often subconsciously. It can also be helpful to talk to people about the topic, to read new material that might be helpful, and to intentionally look for connections in your life. When you finally go back to a piece of writing, you may even be drawn back to it, and you are able to see more clearly and to revise effectively.

Perhaps you do not have the luxury of time and space, or you may simply feel compelled to keep at it. This isn't always a bad thing because momentum has a power of its own. In this case, you might try this method of quick revision. Print out your writing double-spaced and with wide margins. Have extra paper on hand. Using a favorite pen or pencil, revise, delete, and add in the margins and between lines, moving to the back of the page when things get crowded and moving to scratch paper when the back is filled. Do this quickly. Use your momentum. When it's used up, go back to the keyboard, and type in the revisions, making further changes as you go.

When it is time to consider revising your writing, here are some more things to try:

- *Share your writing.* Have others read what you've written. Read for others.
- *Read your writing aloud to yourself or a friend.* Have a friend read the piece to you. Listen for the sound of the language. Listen for meaning. Listen for words that work and words that don't work. In music, when we hear a sour note, even the least musical of us knows that

it's wrong. Our writing also has a melody, a rhythm, and when we hear a clinker, we tend to know it.

• *Sum up what you've written in one or two clear, crisp sentences.* Then reread to see if everything points to that summary statement. If not, or if you find you are unable to summarize, rewrite, omitting dissonant sections or changing the theme.

• *Cut, cut, cut (simplicity, simplicity, simplicity).* Cut the piece to its bare bones. Cut ten pages to five, to two, to one. Think in terms of clarity and brevity. Think minimalism.

• *Ask a trusted teacher or tutor to help.* Even better, if you know a writer, ask her to read what you've written. We often fail to see the problems in our own writing. An expert critical eye can make the difference. Remember, this is not about ego. The best writers are the best partly because they know the value of a good, critical reader during the composing and revising process.

• *Make an outline.* Outlines are not rigid contracts; they're helpers. You can use outlines to lay out a tentative plan, to play with ideas and structure, and to go back to as a piece develops. You might also want to write an outline after a draft is done. That can help you to check the almost finished writing for organization, coherence, and completeness.

We fear change, yet the Tao tells us, "With every movement there is change. With every moment there is alteration" (Chuang Tzu, verse 45). In the Tao we can rejoice in the eternal shifting and beauty of change, in our own creation and recreation, the drafting and revision of our lives, our universe. Our words are not exempt from that change or from the joy of harnessing the great flow in and through our writing.

Take a moment to free write about change. How would you change yourself if you could? How would you change aspects of the world?

7. Writing is unified yet multiplied:

one   multiply

"Maintaining unity is virtuous, for the inner world of thought is
one with the external world of action and of things."
(Tao Te Ching, verse 10)

The Seed, the Tree, the Forest

One of the contradictions of writing is this: good writing emerges from a focused, unified purpose, yet an important objective in the writing process is to explore and, ultimately, to find that focused, unified purpose. In a nutshell: we need to know what we want to write before we write it, but we discover what we want to write by writing. The truth is, of course, that the writer's focus shifts in the act of writing. It may seem that this is not true of personal writing where we are free to go off in all directions, to roam and play, but even this has a unity to it. It may not be to communicate a thesis or tell a story, but to give ourselves inner direction. It may be comprised of many ideas, many dreams, but it is ultimately part of our search for a personal unity.

More formal writing seeks a clearly defined unity, a thematic focus. The Taoist writer will use text to demonstrate the unimpeded flow between the inner and external, to bring one to bear on the other. Consider the kinds of communicative writing we do in school, work, hobbies, activism, and such that need to present a message to readers. It is important that that message be clearly focused on the intended purpose or the result will be obscurity and confusion. The fiction writer who can't decide on a protagonist, problem, or resolution, whose writing is vague, and who tries to inject too many of these into a story, finds that the story wanders and fails to engage readers and, thus, fails as a story. The homeowner who writes a letter of complaint or concern to the company that manufactured his faulty kitchen faucet will need to focus on the specific problem and parts or the company will not be able to remedy the problem. A person who writes a newspaper op-ed piece arguing for the adoption of a flat tax had better focus solely on that theme, or the argument will fall flat.

Finding Unity

Unified writing rarely appears fully formed in a first attempt; writing itself allows us to find that focus, first through the pre-writing, thinking, writing around an idea, or in search of an idea, and the revising process.

Think about how you were taught to write an essay in a conventional English or writing class. Students are taught that the thesis and the essay itself must be unified; in effect, the essay must have a clear controlling idea and focus. This seems obvious to experienced writers, and teachers, familiar with textbooks and style guides, who try to impress this on students in time-honored ways. We emphasize the importance of one main idea and, using arrows and outlines, demonstrate how everything emerges from and goes back to that main idea. This is the conventional way of thinking about unity, and it is certainly valid, but from a Taoist perspective there is a great deal more to it.

We, each of us, are unique, a unified sole being, but we are, at the same time, a part of a much larger unity, of the physical and spiritual universe. Again, let's use the metaphor of a stream, a small creek. It is at once a tiny, singular thing, seemingly inconsequential, a mere trickle. But how can we say which part of the stream is that one thing? What moment in time defines the creek? Of course, every molecule of every drop of water, from beginning to end, is the creek. In a sense, its uniqueness is as real in the microcosm as it is in the macrocosm. When does the stream stop being a unified thing called a creek? Is it when it is absorbed into the banks to be taken in through the roots of the grasses and the trees? Is it when the tiny stream flows into the larger creek then onward into the river, the gulf, the ocean? Or is it when, warmed by the sun, it evaporates into the atmosphere to return again as rain to permeate the soil, moisten tiny seeds and emerge as stems, leaves, blossoms, and fruit? Or is it when the caterpillar eats the leaf, becomes a butterfly, is eaten by the finch, is taken by the cat, which is eaten by the coyote, which is later taken by disease or age to decompose and become part of the soil runoff into a tiny stream—and so on? The essence of the stream has existed long before it was a creek. The life it gives and represents flows out far beyond its humble beginnings and is simply a cyclical perpetuation of the unity.

Writing, too, begins simply, humbly. It is at once a private, isolated activity, a trickle, and a public, communitarian event. We and our words are drops, water molecules in a great universe. We have little choice. Even so, the writer who takes the idea of unity in community to heart, who makes it intentional, learns to write with more power, more life.

We can come together through writing. This is sometimes good and, at other times, not so good. When Thomas Paine wrote his political pamphlets urging fellow American colonists to rise up against the British, his written words had a powerful effect, unifying and giving strength to a revolution that was losing steam. The Bible, the Koran, and the Torah bring millions together, mostly in faith but, unfortunately, often in misguided zeal as well. On a modest level, at the college where I teach, we have tried to unify members of the college and local communities through writing. Each fall, all our freshman writing students read common essays on war and peace, and each student is invited to write a short paper related to the readings and his or her life. Then, in late fall, we hold a conference where, along with invited speakers, students read their papers to audiences of guests, community members, faculty, and other students. On that day, people are brought together as a community of writers to create a potent and positive energy and to plant seeds in one another and the universe that may grow to be significant, and, I hope, peaceful fruit.

There are many opportunities to join with other writers and readers, to commune with one another in a kind of unity that has become rare in our disaffected, fragmented world. Schools, community centers, and bookstores sponsor writing groups where people share their words with one another. Seminars, workshops, and authors' readings bring people together to hear and talk about writing. Open microphones and poetry slams combine performance with text, drawing us from our private writer's rooms and into a community of writers and readers, hearers and seers, in a unified spirit.

When we write with a community of readers and writers, we not only gain the benefits of an attentive audience and sincerely interested readers of our work, but we have the opportunity to become part of others' writing as readers, proofreaders, and participants in the conversation of the text. In rare instances, we become part of a world community, the impact of which can be dramatic and world shaking, even world shifting. Most often we are part of a smaller, more humble writing community. Remember, in the Tao there is no insignificant person, and there is no insignificant good. All great leaps begin with a single spark, a modest seed.

Finding Multiplicity

"Magnify the small; increase the few." (Tao Te Ching, verse 63)

"Great trees grow from the smallest shoots; a terraced garden from a pile of earth, and a journey of a thousand miles begins by taking the initial steps." (verse 64)

The Tao, like life, is full of contradictions. It is internal; it is external. It is unified; it is multiple. Writing is expansive. Like a tiny seed, it begins as a single tiny kernel and grows, first to become a plant, perhaps a tree with numerous branches each sprouting countless leaves and bearing fruit. Each fruit then produces seeds, each capable of becoming a tree with numerous branches, and so on. Humanity is no different. We are the products of parents who are the products of parents, etc. In our writing, an idea begins small, perhaps undefined, and develops into a story, essay, article, song, poem, book, play, diary, and so on. That text then expands. The personal journal or diary may help in our search for answers, for understanding our place in the larger world; consequently, what we find in that very internal writing experience is reflected in our external lives. But even the personal, self-conscious diary belongs to the greater universe.

Just think of the little diary found in an attic in Amsterdam, Holland. The young girl who put her daily thoughts and aspirations on those simple pages did so in all sincerity, in all innocence, the way any young girl might. When, at fifteen years old, Anne Frank died of typhus in Bergen-Belsen concentration camp, few people knew who this young girl was, and few noted her passing. Now, nearly sixty years later, the world knows who Anne Frank was, and the world understands the significance of her experience and the horrors of the Holocaust partly through this little girl's simple words.

Most texts are not as personal as a diary but are written to be read. This reading will directly influence others, even in a subtle way. Words on a page grow according to whom and how many the readers are. In the best instances, the effect extends beyond the text. For example, you probably remember this line: "These are the times that try men's souls." Yet you might not remember its source: Thomas Paine's pamphlet calling colonists to arms against the British. Not that many people have read Paine's entire work, yet they are influenced by it, as is our culture at large.

Writers see their words and ideas multiply as they share writing with friends, family, and classmates. Through writers' reading groups, newsletters, letters to newspapers and journals, online bulletin boards and chat groups, writers can experience the multiplying of their text in the most vivid, literal way. More traditional means of publishing are also becoming more and more accessible to new writers. Online journals cater to all levels of writer, from the rank beginner to the seasoned professional. Local publications, school newspapers, small literary journals, club and hobby newsletters are all eager to publish interesting, relevant writing.

When we write with conviction about our world, we are likely to find that small, unified focused controlling idea and to bring it into the rain, and soil, and sun where, like a seed, it will prosper and multiply.

Take a moment to plant a seed. Write about a small act that can grow into something much larger, a rich fruit.

8. Writing is clarity:

clear

"Pure in heart, like uncut jade, he cleared the muddy water by leaving it alone."
(Tao Te Ching, verse 15)

Seeing the Essence

Religious Taoists describe nine layers of heaven and ten under-worlds, with the heavens further divided. Philosophical Taoists, on the other hand, believe that the Taoist cosmology is largely philosophical, symbolic of existence here on earth. They see in these stories lessons to help us achieve enlightenment in this, our only life. In both the spiritual and philosophical paths the highest levels of heaven and enlightenment are the pure realms called the "Clarities." Although we will not delve into the metaphysical realms of Taoism here, the Taoist aspiration toward a mental and moral clarity can guide us in our approach to writing.

Much in the way meditation can bring clarity to us, writing is a way to both discover and refine our perception of the world. Keeping a journal is recognized for having great therapeutic value in resolving psychological conflict, dealing with stress, and working out issues and questions that crop up in our lives. The very process of writing can help the writer to see more clearly the essence of a problem and explore paths of resolution.

In the more mundane sense, writing is a powerful tool for getting to the kernel of an issue, for finding a missing concept, for *breaking through* in a difficult section of a composition, for creating structure within chaos, and for helping to understand a complex concept or process. In their book *Successful Writing*, Maxine Hairston and Michael Keene write, "Good writing has other qualities too, but clarity comes first, say, way ahead of whatever might come second. It's tempting to think that clear writing must come easily to professional writers, but that's hardly ever the case. Professional writers write more clearly than most other people (although this isn't always the case) because they work at it."

This clarity does not come from memorizing grammatical terms or learning to analyze the structure of a sentence, although each can be interesting and useful in its own right. Clarity in writing comes from communicating effectively. A painter who keeps mixing and adding colors will likely end up with a brown-purple-black mess called mud. In a similar way our attempts to write in a more sophisticated, academic—more correct—way usually result in excessive, ponderous, pompous writing: we choose words that don't mean what we want them to mean, and create long, complicated, confusing sentences that don't end up where we want them to end up.

Too often, people seem to believe that good writing consists of long complex and compound sentences populated with difficult vocabulary and opaque meaning. It's easy to understand why they think this. Much of the writing we hold up as exemplary is anything but, or is taken out of context and seems far more complicated than it truly needs to be. In the first instance, the language used in the law, tax, and medical professions tends to be daunting, and it is almost certainly not good writing. I have a friend named Terry who is a federal judge and a particularly good writer. While he was in law school he made extra money teaching writing classes for lawyers. He says that lawyers, as a rule, are terrible writers, so they tend to hide their meaning behind the awful, thick, confusing language of "legalese."

Of course, we have to recognize the need for a professional language. Jurisprudence and medicine will always include vocabulary that is difficult for the non-expert, but is necessary because of the highly specialized concepts and subject matter of the profession. With much of this overly complicated language, though, the obfuscation is intentional. Lawyers, doctors, and other professionals use it as a way to separate those who've been initiated into the legalese or medical-ese club from the rest of us. The result is added mystery, complexity, and apparent expertise that have most of us looking up to and paying more for these professional services.

In contrast, we achieve clarity as writers when we intentionally write to communicate. The clear writer wants his or her words to be understood in the same way we want to be understood when we're talking to friends. The Taoist writer does this by learning to understand the reader's needs—in a way, by becoming the reader. It matters little how brilliant the prose if the message behind it can't be understood. Most often, what writers think of as brilliant is wordy and pompous. We tend to like our words too much at times, and we forget the reasons for writing them.

Here are just a few simple suggestions for finding clarity in your writing:

1. Put yourself in the place of the reader. Imagine yourself coming to the text fresh, relatively unfamiliar with the topic or background story.
2. Write in active voice instead of passive voice. Passive voice is what might be called backing into a message. When you write, "The car was purchased by the man from Texas," you are writing in passive voice. When you write, "The man from Texas purchased the car," you're in active voice. It just means that the doer is shown to be doing something directly instead of indirectly. Here's another example:

   passive voice—"The song was sung by Ahmad."
   active voice—"Ahmad sang the song."

Writing that strings passive sentences together tends to be dull, the old stereotype of a history book (better than a sleeping pill). It also adds a lot of extra words to a passage, and extra words work against clarity.

3. Don't be afraid to help your reader. If illustrations, charts, notes, and headings make the writing more accessible and help the reader to "get it," use them.
4. Make it simple. Shorter, clearer sentences are easier to read, so they get the message across most effectively.

In the Tao, we follow the middle way, the path of least resistance. In turn, we endeavor to make the way clear of barriers. To this end, the writer should strive for clarity. We can do this first by remembering that we write to communicate with others. The words we choose should be chosen because they will best help the reader understand what we have to say.

Take a moment to look at something you've written. Rewrite it in spare, crisp language. Revise extremely for extreme clarity.

9. Writing is simplicity:

simple

"Better by far to see the simplicity of raw silk's beauty and the uncarved block."
(Tao Te Ching, verse 19)

Small Deeds Multiplied

The Tao brings no more important lesson to writing than the benefit of simplicity. Verse 48 of the Tao Te Ching tells us, "To attain knowledge, add things every day. To attain wisdom, remove things every day." Inexperienced writers typically try to emulate the worst kinds of writing, what they may imagine to be "educated" writing. The result is often verbose, pretentious text, rich with malapropisms and thick, pompous structure. Young writers will often say that they learned to write this way in high school; most likely, though, it is a stage of the writer's development, prompted by the mistaken belief that the most difficult writing to read is the best. As misguided as it is, when writers do this, they are reaching for the treetops, trying out what they see as "good writing." It is a sign of a strong desire to write well. The problem with this "reaching" is that it can become habit. In the end, writers seem strangely determined to write the kinds of prose they hate to read. The most successful might go on to perpetuate this awful stuff, and the cycle continues. Many others go through life thinking they are poor writers because they can't quite master the overdone prose. For a lucky few, the bad habits will fall away with time and practice, but it's best not to leave our writing to chance.

The Tao Te Ching's call for simplicity parallels the writing instructor's advice, to strive for simplicity and clarity in writing. English author Arthur Quiller-Couch originated one of the purest rules of writing you will ever hear. He advised, "If you require a practical rule of me, I will present you with this: Whenever you feel an impulse to perpetrate a piece of exceptionally fine writing, obey it—wholeheartedly—and delete it before you send in your manuscript to press. Murder your darlings." The Bisy Backsons of the world need the clutter. "Emptiness," writes

Benjamin Hoff in *The Tao of Pooh*, "reminds them of loneliness. Everything has to be filled in." The writer who peels away the layers of complexity will find a kernel of meaning inside and can then, if the task calls for it, develop levels of complex meaning with clarity.

The Tao Te Ching tells us, "Prepare for what is difficult while it is still easy. Deal with what is big while it is still small" (verse 48). The writer who understands the power of simplicity is able to create the longer works that seem so intimidating at first glance. Anyone who has written a lengthy book, dissertation, or other major work understands that writers must begin with small steps and build up a work piece by piece, yet few beginning writers understand that these tomes are pieced together, often over years of stops and starts, trial and error. Verse 93 of the Tao Te Ching tells us "It is the way of nature that even difficult things are done with ease, and great acts made up of smaller deeds. The sage achieves greatness by small deeds multiplied." The Tao also tells us "A journey of a thousand miles begins by taking the initial steps" (verse 64). Consider the simplicity of the Tao Te Ching itself. It is not an impressive volume in size and weight, not even filling one hundred pages of a modern paperback. Moreover, it isn't presented in the complicated, flowery language we might expect from a "great book," one which we tend to think is meant for expert readers. In fact, it is accessible and meaningful to any average reader. Yet it is a work of such breadth and depth that its brief contents have captured imaginations for thousands of years and have influenced societies and thinkers from Confucius to Emerson to the Dalai Lama. It, like much that we value, is profound in its simplicity. In his book *Walden*, Henry David Thoreau writes:

Our life is frittered away by detail. An honest man has hardly need to count more than his ten fingers, or in extreme cases he may add his ten toes, and lump the rest. Simplicity, simplicity, simplicity! I say, let your affairs be as two or three, and not a hundred or a thousand; instead of a million count half a dozen, and keep your accounts on your thumb-nail. In the midst of this chopping sea of civilized life, such are the clouds and storms and quicksands and thousand-and-one items to be allowed for, that a man has to live, if he would not founder and go to the bottom and not make his port at all, by dead reckoning, and he must be a great calculator indeed who succeeds. Simplify, simplify.

Simplicity and a Fear of Tomes

As with much in life, the first step in understanding the power of simplicity in writing is to understand our perceptions of writing. How often do we hear, or say, "Oh, I could never write a book. It's too long." It is intimidating, yet most of us have written books—we simply haven't had the pages and chapters bound into a volume. Letters and e-mails are short, but consider how many missives you have written over the years. Consider the pages and pages you've composed for English, history, and social studies teachers. Many of us have penned countless stories or poems, and many others have written page after page of proposals and reports. Odds are, you have written a book, but you've done so in brief, simple snippets. Of course, your letter or memo book may not win the Pulitzer or Nobel Prize, but that doesn't matter. What matters is that you have done it—almost effortlessly, unconsciously, simply. And, you can do it again, this time with intention. Authors do not write a complete book in an instant or a day. They write it in increments. Once we understand this, the task of creating a book becomes much easier to understand and undertake. We write one word at a time. We can't expect to write a Tao Te Ching, and the Bible, Koran, and Torah are unlikely to add new chapters, but it serves us well to remember that, just as a world of forests, humanity, and beauty resides in tiny seeds, a world of meaning is born of a well-chosen word.

Take a moment to write. Jot down everything you know about a complicated concept, issue, or problem. Simplify the language you use to discuss it. Then describe the complicated idea in the simplest terms and shortest, clearest sentences you can manage.

10. Writing is personal:

person

"Knowing others is wisdom; knowing the self is enlightenment."
(Tao Te Ching, verse 33)

A Path to the Soul

Personal writing has gotten a bad name, and it's often for good reason. It can be easy to misunderstand the role of personal writing in the writer's repertoire. The Taoist writer accepts the need we all have to understand ourselves, and personal writing can help us do that. Furthermore, it is in this understanding of self that we begin to understand others. Journals and diaries offer us a chance to express our fondest desires and deepest fears. We tend to keep them hidden away in dresser drawers and on the top shelf of the closet. On occasion, a unique diary or journal can become public literature as did the poignant diaries of Civil War soldiers or the heartbreaking *The Diary of Anne Frank*. More often, however, they are meant to be kept private. For example, the stereotypical teenager's diary is a painful read for most of us. It is certainly important as a private, personal record, and it is undoubtedly profound to the writer, but it is not a public document. It is perhaps the most personal of texts. The journal may be just as private but is often a more mundane narrative of events, reactions to readings, notes about the progress of a project and such. In each case, however, this personal, inward looking kind of writing informs and enriches our public writing.

In the early 1970s, writing experts began to trumpet the power of personal writing in our quest to learn and teach writing. These "expressivists" believed that young writers would develop in skill and correctness if just given the opportunity and time to write a lot. They soon discovered that, although they were on the right track, young writers needed more than their own expressivist aspirations to become polished writers. Writers need a combination of desire, practice, and guidance. Even so, the private, self-sponsored kinds of writing we tend to do are profoundly important in our development as writers. Think about it: young writers rarely pour their emotions into book reports, or spend hours or their own time creating research papers for social studies class. Writers find inspiration in personal kinds of writing. Ultimately, it is something inside of each of us that makes us writers. Thus personal writing is not sufficient, but it is necessary.

The Healing Word

The Tao is accessible to each of us individually. Indeed, we must listen for ourselves to hear it, to find enlightenment. In the same way, each of us has a unique voice, each carrying a personal message that can flow into the universe through our writing.

Personal writing can be deeply therapeutic. In her book, *When Your Heart Speaks, Take Good Notes: The Healing Power of Writing,* Susan Borkin describes a path of healing through personal writing. In her chapter entitled "The Tao of Writing," Borkin says, "When we use writing as a tool for awareness and healing, we find the outcome, the written word, to be useful, but frequently not as useful as the process of writing itself. Personal writing of this nature is intentional writing. Its deepest intention is to heal" (from *www.susanborkin.com*). Borkin's personal writing is free of rules, free of barriers, and, unlike most of the writing we are discussing here, free of outside readers. The purpose, says Borkin, is "to be as honest, as clear, and as deeply connected to your soul as possible."

Borkin's personal writing may seem to be just a kind of introspective, lonely writing in which the writer tries to create a protective cocoon, to hide from the outside. Yet the result is just the opposite, as such writing participates in a healing that emanates outward into the greater universe. It inevitably bears fruit in the world. This most free of free writing also helps the author become a more proficient, stronger writer. So, by virtue of the rich introspection inherent in personal writing, the writer is moved further along a path of writing competency, self-knowledge, and personal healing.

Take a moment to write. Keep a journal beside your bed, and each night spend a few minutes jotting down thoughts of the day and hopes for the next.

11. Writing is universal:

universal

"Man's laws should follow natural laws, just as nature gives rise to physical laws, whilst following from universal law, which follows the Tao."
(Tao Te Ching, verse 25)

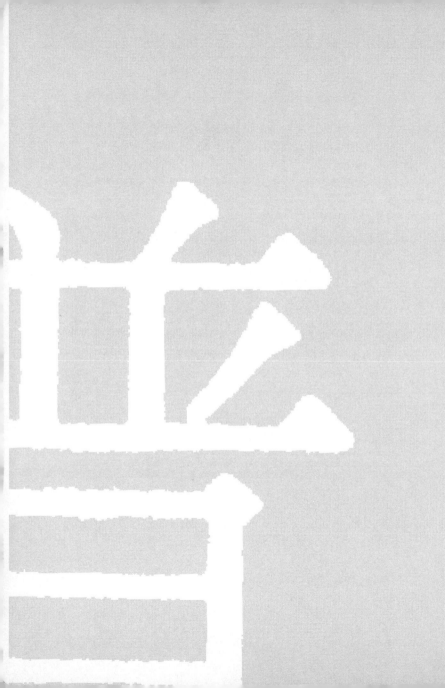

A Path to the Universe

Lao Tzu wrote, "Trees and animals, humans and insects, flowers and birds, these are active images of the subtle energies that flow from the stars throughout the universe. Meeting and combining with each other and the elements of the Earth, they give rise to all living things. The superior person understands this and understands that her own energies play a part in it" (Walker, 43).

The writer who refuses to revise because she so loves her words is like a young woman sitting in a corner at a party, head tucked down into a guitar, singing and playing quietly to herself. Inevitably, although someone hears the music, the very nature of this lonely experience, is colored, perhaps clouded by the sullen, introverted nature of the song. Better to sing out, to send the song out strong and open to the other partygoers, to offer the music as it is meant to be given. Writing is universal in that it is part of a dialogue with our inner and outer worlds. Whether that dialogue blossoms fully in the world or seeps out in hushed innuendo, incomplete and uncertain, is up to the writer.

Many—perhaps most—of those of us who are writers are introverted to some extent. We fear letting go, letting the music and the words flow freely out into the universe to blend our energy with the energies of others, "of all living things," in a way that offers truth. Of course, we can't avoid being a part of this universal community, but we can and must have a voice in the shape our participation takes and the impact it has.

The Tao tells us that we can consciously choose to send prayers into the universe. Even today, Chinese Taoists send messages and prayers to ancestors each Chinese New Year. They write their missives on scraps of paper and, along with a kind of paper money printed just for this purpose, set it on fire, sending their good wishes and desires aloft via the smoke.

Closer to home and to our purposes, we can tap the universality of writing through community. In every case, the writer is a small part of a great community of ideas and writings. We literally sit on the shoulders of others, some giants, most like us. Our writing emerges from our relationships, what we read, what our culture has imposed, and it leads to the real or implied audience. In this way, writing is always a dialogue or a piece of a great conversation.

Writers and writing teachers have known the power of community for many years. We write with others in graduate school; and newsrooms around the world are noisy, messy writing communities in which writers give to and take from one another before sending their pieces off to the editors and, most important, to that even greater dialogue with the readers.

Many young writers are surprised by this. They tend to go off into their corners to write in solitude and, like the lonely singer, end up creating text that reflects that experience. The writing is often insular, and over the long term, stunted. Writing evolves through writing, writing, and more writing. And it develops through reading, sharing, thinking, trying, trying again, creating, recreating, reading, sharing, talking, writing, writing, and writing.

For a number of years, I've been meeting with a group of colleagues and friends to share the kinds of writing we all do for our work in higher education. One writer will distribute a piece a week or so before our get-together. Everyone reads, highlights, and jots down comments and questions. Then we sit down together with coffee and tea and we talk about the work. We offer suggestions, praise, criticism, and consider where the writer might publish the piece. I've read and discussed pieces on spirituality in prison culture, toxic hot-spots in our region, and giants in English literary history. The important thing about this exercise is that we do it. Merely by doing it, most of the time the author discovers a new angle, a way to restructure, to revise simply in the act of talking about the writing with others. Most writers understand that their work grows within this broad conversation. We put our writing out into the community, sending it into the wider universe, in order to become better, more aware writers and to offer our words to others. By virtue of this humble offering, we gain immeasurably.

Writing, then, is a consciously universal form of conversation, but it is also universal in that it is not exclusive to those we call "writers." Non-literate cultures have written since time began using pictographs and symbols to help them understand and interpret their worlds. Paulo Freire, the Brazilian activist and teacher, saw this extended text in the peasant classes of his country, and tapped into their symbolic culture to develop his revolutionary and groundbreaking literacy program.

Ultimately nature itself and the universe write the most marvelous texts of all—the symbols we worship, cherish, fear, and wonder at and which define so much of whom and what we are. This is writing on a grand, one could say "universal" scale. It is the flow of the Tao.

Take a moment to write and read with others. Join a writer's group. Start a group. It is even possible to join online writer's clubs over the Internet.

12. Writing is open-ended:

endless

"The Tao is forever undefined."
(Tao Te Ching, verse 32)

"It is the nature of the Tao that even though used continuously, it is replenished naturally, never being emptied and never being over-filled, as is a goblet which spills its contents upon the ground."
(verse 4)

The Evolving Word

Young writers are taught that a story has a beginning, a middle, and an end. The revision process culminates with a final draft. When an essay, article, or book is ready for publication, we claim that it is done. Closure is important to us humans. Yet, the concept of being done is an illusion that even we in the West, while claiming otherwise, don't buy wholesale. For all we know, and based on every bit of actual evidence, death may be the literal end of us, but most human beings cling to religions and philosophies that promise us we will live on. We're sorry to see a good book end, we wait for the sequels to our favorite movies, and we hang on to fantastic, even destructive dreams and obsessions long after they're proven fruitless.

The truth is we really don't like endings after all—but not to worry. The very nature of the Tao assures us that we exist in an endless ebb and flow. Endings are illusory on the micro and macro levels. That, of course, includes writing. We complete texts because we live in a temporal world. It would be impractical and silly to suggest that we never see our writing as finished. Still, what we write and how it enables us to communicate our sense of the universe is open-ended. We evolve constantly and, as we experience life, our ideas also evolve. None of us is stagnant. When we recognize and value the energy of impermanence, we grow. Like it or not, we are perpetual motion machines.

Writing evolves and is, in reality, never "just so." The finest authors will say, "I wish I had taken this out or used that instead of this," or, "If only that character had done that." We want the luxury of making our writing better, or at least different.

The Internet has created a kind of writing that allows for endless additions and revisions in writing and reading text.

Hypertext is a term that describes the almost endless links and pathways we can follow in reading a text on the World Wide Web (WWW). Hypertext is a layers-deep system of nodes and connections in which one word in a text can lead to screen after screen of related information. For example, an introductory paragraph on the writer and philosopher Michel Foucault might summarize aspects of his childhood, his education, his creativity, his sexuality, and his later work. Each of these topics, then, is highlighted on the screen, and when the reader clicks on the topic, a new screen is opened that provides more detailed information on the chosen topic, say, childhood. A short biography might contain more "hot button" words that will lead to more screens giving more and differently related information, leading perhaps into other nodes—education, sexual development, experiences during the war, etc. Before long, a reader can find herself completely outside of the original topics.

Many of us have experienced the differences between reading conventional text and hypertext when we've begun reading an article or a topical web page and, before we realize it, we've jumped countless sites away having been drawn far from our original text through the web's penchant for tangents. This may or may not be a good thing for someone who is trying to focus on a topic, but it illustrates the open-ended potential of the Web in a graphic way. Of course, the Web is finite but, in theory, a text could be written and rewritten infinitely. In any case, the Web is constantly shifting and changing.

Of course, we don't need computer technology to show us that text is always new, always changing. Some would say that the Bible, in its many forms, is an evolving work. The original books were not in English, Spanish, or Mandarin, or even within a single language. Texts differ from version to version, revision to revision. The books included in the King James Bible, for example, are a select part of the total writing found and attributed to Biblical sources. Whenever a new translation, a vernacular text, a children's Bible, etc., is created, words change, meaning is altered, and the work evolves.

The Tao Te Ching is no different. I've read half a dozen versions—and obviously there are many more—and each was translated and interpreted. Text evolves.

William Zinsser writes, "A piece of writing must be viewed as a constantly evolving organism." What this means for us as writers is that our writing will change by our hand, by the hands of others, and always by the reading. Each interpretation is new and each reading alters the text. When we understand this, we can begin to harness that inevitable change, to recognize that it is not only useful but desirable. In a practical sense, the open-ended nature of what we write contributes to the broad textual conversation, to a great body of written work. This isn't restricted to great authors and well-known scholars. Love letters can track the path of romance and, too often, of heartbreak and tragedy. Memos can reflect an ongoing, evolving conversation and process, and the kinds of writing we do for work can take on lives of their own. (Consider the plight of corrupt CEOs who have found their writing used against them in court.) The laws of evolution also apply to the writing we do in school, in our research papers, short stories, and dissertations. A student may want to use something he'd written for another class to develop a piece for a writing assignment. In my opinion, it is precisely this kind of interdisciplinary linking that makes for great scholars. This is growth; this is evolution. It's a process that taps into the natural continuum of the Tao that reminds us that we and the universe are interconnected, seamless, and ongoing.

Take a moment to write a short narrative, a story without an ending. Leave the final sentence unfinished. Then, each day for a week (or longer if you wish), continue from that point and, when you reach the end, leave the final sentence unfinished. This also works well with variations of free writing.

Part 3

Applying the
Tao to Writing

Te: The Tao of Writing
Is an Ethical Way

"The Heavenly Tao has no favorites: It raises up the good."

(Tao Te Ching, verse 79)

"The highest goodness is like water.

Water easily benefits all things without struggle.

Yet it abides in places that men [people] hate.

Therefore, it is like the Tao.

For dwelling, the Earth is good.

For the mind, depth is good.

The goodness of giving is in the timing.

The goodness of speech is in honesty.

In government, self-mastery is good.

In handling affairs, ability is good."

(verse 8)

The Virtuous Way

The Dalai Lama has said, "Dangerous consequences will follow when politicians and rulers forget moral principles" (Dalai Lama, *A Human Approach to Word Peace*, DharmaNet online edition). The Taliban in Afghanistan destroy ancient Buddhas and kill fellow citizens in the name of Islam. Hindus kill and are killed by their Moslem neighbors in their zeal over so-called sacred sites and temples. Israelis and Palestinians slaughter one another over what they deem to be a sacred hill and ancient land claims. Certain zealous Christians put a price on the heads of pro-choice physicians and workers. Claiming to be soldiers of Allah, al-Qaeda terrorists attack Western governments and civilians of all nationalities and religions. Western leaders confidently claim, "God is on our side!" as they embark on retaliatory or aggressive adventures. In every case, God is called upon to support hatred and brutality. This is too often the face of religion and has been for much of history.

In the secular realm, corporate leaders from Enron, WorldCom., and many other companies lie and steal, enriching themselves while their trusting employees, investors, and customers lose their money, jobs, and their meager savings and retirement funds. A pharmacist dilutes chemotherapy drugs to increase his profit margin while cancer patients struggle to defeat the disease and, lacking the medication they believe they are getting, die.

Even in what we would think are the most high-minded settings, we human animals are often a particularly bad lot. We commit crimes, hide sins, and are generally unethical as a matter of course. To counteract this, we tend to appeal to a higher power or, more specifically, to religion, yet we find that even there, in the cathedrals, the mosques, the synagogues, and temples, this ideal of goodness, this purity of spirit and intent, seems to escape us.

This is not to say that religion is bad. In fact, the fundamental philosophies of religions are, as a rule, high-minded and truly aim for the betterment of humankind. The problems come about in the usual way. Human beings interpret, organize, and administer religion. They may mess things up intentionally, or they may have the best intentions in mind, but corruption is inevitable and is all the more damaging because so many followers come to believe that the abuses are the will of God.

Tao is not a religion in the sense that it does not proffer a deity or judge people to be good or bad. It is more a way of living, a philosophy of being. Although it lacks the mystical trappings of the Jewish, Catholic, or Moslem faiths, its way is virtuous.

As the Tao means the Way, in Lao Tzu's Tao Te Ching, *Te* represents virtue. Taoism is not a philosophy of good and evil in the way conventional religions tend to be. Even so, adherence to the Tao is, by necessity, adherence to a virtuous path. Most specifically, as Ted Kardish has written, "Te refers to the fact that all things contain an inherent power or strength that comes from their own essential being or true inner nature" (Kardash, 1). That "true inner nature" is, according to Lao Tzu, "an inherent goodness." To help us manifest this virtue, Lao Tzu gives us "three treasures: compassion, frugality or balance, and humility" (Kardash, 2). These are not the characteristics demonstrated by the corrupt CEOs, heads of state, and religious leaders mentioned earlier.

The Tao of writing is ethical. Chuang Tzu says, "Who knows the Tao must get to principle. Who gets to principle will stand enlightened about power. Whoever is enlightened about power won't be damaged by things. Those who get to the Power of Virtue can't be burned by fire or drowned in water . . . Don't let gain lead you astray, toward fame. Be careful! Guard your heart, don't lose it. This is called getting back to the truth" (Hamill and Seaton, 88–89). The power of the Tao is in truth. Writing can offer a way into that truth. This is not a new idea, since authors have been following this principle for thousands of years.

We are accustomed to thinking about writing as authoritative and, thus, true. This elevated sense, this authority of the written word has a long tradition. To ancient Egyptians, writing held an aura of magic. To early Europeans, it was a tool of the spirit and power. Controlled mostly by the Catholic Church, it had the imprimatur of the Papacy and, by extension, of God upon it. Even today our most cherished beliefs are contained within the pages of "great books." Our laws are ensconced in impressive, leather-bound law books; our religious wisdom emanates from holy books; our medical and scientific knowledge is put down in books of complex theory; our most profound ideas of ancient and modern times exist in stories and philosophical treatises set down in print. We still find that words in black and white hold more credibility than the spoken word.

And yet, even the holiest, most lawful, most scientifically profound texts are often manipulated and frequently wrong. Consider the early writing on genetics and on human intelligence. Well-respected scholars and public leaders fell in line lockstep behind the most specious pronouncements about ethnicity and intellect. No matter that research on race was shoddy or nonexistent. No matter that many exponents of these white-superiority theories were well-known racists with clear self interests. In spite of the obvious lies behind the words, the work published on the inferiority of this or that ethnic group was taken up enthusiastically by a public eager to justify and rationalize bankrupt policy. The Taoist writer must follow the flow of ideas and reason, and must do so in an ethical way. That is to say, to write, speak, or act to support what is wrong contradicts the natural tenets of the Tao. The Taoist writer must write with compassion, balance, humility, and a firm adherence to truth.

The compassionate writer strives to understand others' needs and to give whatever it is that will most help the reader and most fairly treat the subject. The Taoist writer creates text that does not take from or hurt but that gives and heals. For example, such a writer would not be involved in a negative political campaign, would not alter information in a report to give a company a dishonest advantage in the market, and would not write to family, friends, or even enemies in an unethical, intentionally hurtful manner. The Taoist writer will use words to enhance harmony and build up rather than to tear down.

The balanced writer does not seek to take unfair advantage of others but seeks to understand and accommodate the values and needs even of those with opposing points of view. The balanced writer does not attack with vehemence but concedes the validity of another's position. The balanced writer recognizes that she too does not hold the key to virtue and goodness and truth, that the path of the Tao is not simplistic. A favorite writing assignment in many high school classes asks students to argue an issue from the other side, a viewpoint at odds with their own. A pro-choice individual might have to argue against a woman's right to an abortion, and a pro-gun person to argue in favor of restricting firearm ownership. In creative writing classes, students might be asked to create villains from heroes and heroes from villains, to ask their characters to behave in ways that go against the author's preconceptions and instincts, which cut against the grain. Fictional characters must be balanced to be believable, neither all good nor all bad.

In the same way, our nonfiction writing must be balanced to be credible. This is not to say that as a writer you must divorce yourself from conviction or must follow a rigid formula, but we are most ethical and just when we acknowledge the duality of human existence and circumstance. In order to do this, a writer must be willing to see more than one side, must possess a degree of humility.

The humble writer does not see herself or her beliefs as the ultimate truth, as being right to the exclusion of others. The humble writer respects those who make up her audience and, while addressing them with confidence, recognizes that they will judge what is written according to their needs, influences, and unique perspective. This writer appeals to the reader's needs. For example, some years ago I bought a six-pack of a locally brewed beer (Yes, I like beer. I even brew it from time to time.). I soon realized that one twelve-ounce can was lighter than the rest. I poured the contents into a measuring cup and discovered that it held only eight ounces. On a whim, I wrote a light-hearted letter to the company, pointing out that the can in question was in fact, one-third less filling than the others and that, although it tasted fine, eight ounces was just not enough of such a wonderful lager. I also noted that the error could be an indication of serious problems with their bottling equipment. The letter was friendly and helpful while also pointing out, diplomatically, that I hadn't gotten what I had paid for. It was a letter of complaint, but it was not a complaining or demanding letter. The reaction to this, and to many other similar letters I've written over the years, was not the reaction we usually expect from a letter of complaint. The brewmaster himself telephoned to tell me that everybody in the company loved the letter and said that they were still laughing. He also thanked me for pointing out a potentially serious problem in their processing plant, invited me for a personal tour of the brewery, and sent me two cases of my favorite brew.

The reaction to my letter shouldn't be a surprise. As the saying goes, "You catch more flies with honey than with vinegar." You can also make more friends and reach more goals with humility and generosity than with arrogance. The Taoist writer's approach to text is compassionate, balanced, and humble. In writing, as in all things, the Way is a virtuous path.

The Tao Is a Peaceful Way

"The wise man acts at one with the Tao, for he knows that it is here that peace is found."

(Tao Te Ching, verse 35)

Beyond Partisan Politics

I hadn't planned on including a section on peace and the Tao. It seemed out of context, apart from the thesis of this work. After all, I'm writing about writing here. Then it became more and more important in my mind to rethink that posture. One night recently, I was driving to a small coffeehouse to sing at an open microphone evening I frequent. On the way, I began thinking about a news item I saw on television. The announcer began, "Here now in silence we honor some of the service men and women who have died in Iraq." This was followed by a poignant montage of Americans who have been killed in action. By the time I reached the club, I had penned a song that begins, "Here in silence we honor you, the good, the brave, the frightened too, who died for what they never knew. We give to you our love." I performed the song that night. We need to realize that, as writers and thinking, caring human beings, we cannot ignore conflict, and we cannot discount the promise of peace. It is part of life, and it is part of the Tao.

The Tao is not partisan, not Democratic, Republican, Socialist, Communist, Fascist, or Independent. The Tao is itself— the Tao is the way. It has existed long before the petty bickering of partisan politics and wars, and it will exist long after.

Te, the ethics of Tao, must guide us to a peaceful way, and because our writing is inseparable from our lives, it must reflect and project the peaceful Tao.

Simplicity and Peace

Ours is a stressed-out, tense, hyperactive, hyper-busy culture. We work constantly, eat poorly, relax in mindless sometimes destructive, often unhealthy ways, and seem determined to 135 complicate our world and lives as much as we possibly can. The Tao provides patterns of simplicity that help us become centered and allow us to create our own life patterns for living in the world without, or at least with far less of the craziness and resulting stress of modern life. This centering opens a space in which we can feel at peace. Diane Dreher, author of *The Tao of Inner Peace*, writes, "Seeking simplicity in a world of impermanence is quite a challenge. Yet scaling down and becoming more conscious of how we use things creates greater peace individually and collectively" (Dreher, 78).

Just as all politics are local, all peace is local and begins within ourselves and our lives. But our individual actions and attitudes, like a ripple on the surface of a pond, radiate outward both in metaphysical and physical terms. For example, when we choose to live in a smaller house, drive a smaller car (or better yet, walk, ride a bike, or take public transportation), buy fresh foods, and use energy-efficient products, we, of course, have an effect upon local workers, businesses, and such, but we also impact world trade, fuel production and prices, food packaging, chemical output, employment, environmental pollution, and infinitely more.

Simplicity is a tool for peace because it fosters cooperation and coexistence in place of competition and separation. Our writing can do the same. Words of peace create harmony between people, neighborhoods, and cultures. As writers, we strive for simplicity and clarity, to avoid misunderstanding, to promote cooperation. Writers often write to persuade. If this is done in a spirit of hatred or violence, it creates a ripple of energy that threatens to amplify and perpetuate hatred and violence, bitter fruit indeed. Writing for peace and harmony will bear the sweet fruit of peace.

It isn't hard to do, and the writer who follows the Tao need not follow any specific rules other than that the writing be toward a peaceful end. Many political activists seem to feel that to be involved and sincere, people must follow a pro-scribed path: they must belong to a certain organization or organizations, must read certain materials, and must write in certain ways for specific causes. In other words, peace activists are like everybody else. Like conservatives, moderates, liberals, preachers, thieves, politicians, dentists, butchers, bakers, and candlestick makers, they are often opinionated and sometimes humorless and overbearing. I once lived in a very small com-munity in Wisconsin in which the vast majority of citizens were pro-environment and anti-war. In fact, the county had officially identified itself as an anti-nuclear zone. One summer a local environmental group invited a well-known environmental-action organization to hold a rally and concert in the town. The environmental activists came in and proceeded to preach to the local folks. Their hard-nosed, in your face, autocratic, humorless assault on the community alienated many who, frankly, were in agreement with most of the group's objectives. Of course, many activists are instead warm and humble in the way they relate to the world. In any case, it seems clear that peace does not come as a result of arrogance and enforced ideology.

The Taoist writer then must choose his own path and must not be cowed by others' opinions on what it means to write for peace. In the simplest, most humble terms, we write for peace each time we express peaceful thoughts and aspira-tions in writing. Affirmations, diary and journal entries, peaceful musings of any kind, add to the flow of peaceful energy in the world, and the writer who goes no further than this is writing for peace.

Of course, it is hard to keep our convictions to ourselves, so even the most introverted writer will often send messages of peace to friends and family through e-mail and letters. This is the kind of text that can have an immediate impact on others' attitudes and behavior.

At the next level, the peaceful writer will seek a broader audience, even in modest terms. As a writer, you might recite poems, read stories, or sing your own songs at a local café. To reach even more people, you can publish your work in a number of ways. You may publish in club or community newsletters, local newspapers, or in online forums. In each case, you have the ability as a writer to touch others, sometimes many others, and the impact is positive.

Once we move outside of ourselves and consciously reach out to others with a peaceful message, we become leaders. At that point, we can take a peaceful message to many others and, according to the principles of the Tao, the message will multiply, and many who we touch will become influences for peace.

It is not difficult to become part of the stream, the flow of peaceful writing, but, as Diane Dreher reminds us in *The Tao of Inner Peace*, it is not easy to work for harmony in a harsh world. She says, "Facing a world of conflict and confusion, we must remember to stay centered, to maintain our inner balance" (Dreher, 189). She adds, "We must never let a cause, and organization, a relationship so completely eclipse our lives that we forget who we are." We can achieve that balance through reminding ourselves that we must let ourselves flow in synch with the universe, through meditation, and through our writing. We should not be distracted from that simple truth.

The Writing Space

"Even the most abstract mind is affected by
the surroundings of the body. No one is immune
to the impressions that impinge on the senses
from outside."

(Mihaly Csikszentmihalyi,
*Creativity: Flow and the Psychology of
Discovery and Invention*, 127)

The Tao of Tidiness

It is no secret that writers are most productive in the right space or spaces. Mihaly Csikszentmihalyi writes in his book *Creativity* about the importance of environments that inspire. He describes writing "in a small stone cell, seven feet square, with two French windows looking out over the eastern branch of Lake Como, in northern Italy, near the foothills of the Alps" (133). Writing textbooks advise writers to write in a place that is quiet and uncluttered, to make the place one's own with personal items, photographs, posters, music, etc., and to find tools that are pleasing and comfortable. Even though I am a writing teacher, I still struggle with my own writing spaces. My office is often piled with student papers, notes, assignments, textbooks, committee work, proposals, memos, and everything else that makes up a modern English professor's environment.

So, as I began to write this, I also began to reconfigure my office and my way of working to eliminate unnecessary paper and clutter. Instinct and experience tell me that an uncluttered environment will allow me to approach my work and my own writing with a clear mind, helping me to be more organized, more productive. Although, as I begin the task, I'm fully aware that I want to approach the change in a distinctly Taoist fashion, I also understand what seems obvious, that physical distractions are likely to distract me from my work and to create a certain level of unease. I depend on being able to focus, to concentrate on a task. Thus my goal is not expressly to make my office a Taoist temple. It just so happens that the Taoist approach to spatial design makes sense.

Feng Shui for the Writer

A major aspect of the growing success of Eastern ideas in the West, particularly in the United States and Canada, is the adaptability of a given philosophy. The question is not whether or not feng shui can work in the United States. It is working and has become incredibly popular, as is evident by the proliferation of titles on library and bookstore shelves. Feng shui practitioners and consultants are popping up everywhere, and they are having an impact. It may be tempting to see feng shui as another half-baked pseudo-science/pseudo-philosophy, followed by only the fringe of American society, but nothing could be farther from the truth. Homeowners, small businesses, even corporations are following the precepts of feng shui to improve their environments and, in the latter case, their productivity. Victoria's Secret, the popular lingerie store, is said to have employed a feng shui consultant since the early nineties. Other companies that have consciously incorporated feng shui principles in their design and workplace organization and decoration include such major firms as CitiBank and Chase Manhattan Bank. This is not to say there is something magical or metaphysical in feng shui, although some practitioners would disagree. Feng shui is, in its most fundamental form, a philosophy of balance and flow in design. It is a philosophy of shape, color, sense of space, and the energy and moods that emerge from the combination of these attributes. However we interpret the truth behind the philosophy, feng shui offers great possibilities for the writer's space.

This book is not intended to provide a primer on feng shui. For that, you can read such works as Terah Katherine Collins' *The Western Guide to Feng Shui* and Lillian Too's *The Fundamentals of Feng Shui*, or check your library or bookstore for other fine titles.

The Internet is also a good resource. The intention, rather, is to offer here a loosely Taoist point of view on the writer's space and tools which can help us become more creative, productive writers, because attention to space and, particularly, to balance will make us better writers. In fact, it will improve our lives in every way.

Feng shui literally means "wind and water." It is the Taoist way of organizing space, the places in which we live and work, to create a positive flow, a harmony. Like wind and water, the energy in our environments should flow effortlessly and positively. The writer is far more likely to thrive in such an atmosphere than when such harmony is absent.

This has little to do with metaphysics (although some would argue the point). This approach to spatial arrangement and planning is, at its base, a practical way to create balance and harmony in our living spaces. Even those who see it as nothing more than spatial common sense, are likely to acknowledge its value as an organizing guide.

Let's look at the writer's space and introduce the concept of feng shui from a purely practical perspective. Writers often have to find a quiet library, dining room table, or cafe booth to get work done, even though they may have a well-equipped office or study expressly designated for their writing. The places we are supposed to use for writing too often end up as deposits of notes, check stubs, magazines, pens and pencils, books, old mail and, in my case, odd bits of recording equipment, drawing pads, and such. Most of us simply can't write in the midst of the clutter and distractions of our familiar places.

Clutter

Who's to say what qualifies as clutter? Some writers claim that their work thrives in chaos. In most cases, it's rarely as chaotic as it might appear. Even the chronically messy tend to have

143

order in the piles that surround them. The truth is most of us crave order, largely because it can be so hard to achieve.

I live amid stacks of student papers, notes, books and journals, memos, flyers and such—a debris field that would put a frown on the merriest of "Merry Maids." I manage to work in this crowded environment until it seems to build to a critical mass, and then I start shoveling, clearing every flat space until I can breathe—figuratively. The truth is, I rarely write at my desk in my office. Instead I write at the kitchen or dining room table in my home. Unlike most of my house, the dining room and kitchen tables are open, flat spaces in good light, usually free of clutter. Both rooms have large bay windows overlooking several acres of creeping charley and bits of lawn under giant oak, maple, and towering pine trees. I find the extended space almost meditative. Whatever it is that creates the particular environment that is so conducive to writing, in my case it is spacious, green, and ordered.

Clutter is distraction. The flow of writing is inevitably stopped, interrupted by the noise of clutter. The photographs in Jill Krementz's *The Writer's Desk* of noted authors and their workspaces bear me out. Writers are, for the most part, a tidy lot. We realize that the universe flows regardless of a sink full of last night's dirty supper dishes, the hiccups of politics in a small town, or volcanoes erupting off the coast of Hawaii, but most writers are not so resilient and must write in an ordered universe. Of course, it may be a quirky, on the edge of chaos kind of order, but order it is nonetheless.

In effect, most of us concentrate better, focus better, and write better in an organized, well-lighted niche.

Distraction

We live in a time characterized by distraction. Televisions, radios, stereos and boom boxes, and computers all vie for our attention, often simultaneously. We can watch programming dedicated to sports, history, science fiction, news, comedy, cartoons, religion, nature, cooking, soap operas, music, sex, finance, movies, and just about anything else that catches somebody's fancy, and whenever we like. Cable and satellite television hookups provide forty, eighty, one hundred and fifty or more stations, and households from a trailer in the Arizona desert, to a military barracks in Norway, to a rooftop in Baghdad sprout satellite dishes drawing everything from around-the-clock warfare, to music videos, to soccer, golf and curling, to *Andy Griffith* and *I Love Lucy*. And when we leave our homes, we are accosted by even more noise. Ubiquitous loudspeakers attack our senses on public transportation and in public places and pipe uninspired versions of the latest uninspired musical trend into more and more corners of our lives while, often, teens pump out their own musical jams and everything blends in a grand, noisy cacophony. Cars roar through formerly sedate neighborhoods pounding the air and testing our patience with hyper-amplified, super-bass systems.

Invasive bits of our world, annoying noise, garish images, disruption, and distraction are everywhere. The distractions we find appealing are even more present and, often, more insidious. People, pets, loved ones, telephone calls, books, mail, and the countless other projects begging for our attention usually get it.

It is hard to avoid this byproduct of what we've euphemistically come to call progress, and the slower, more contemplative places of the world seem intent upon following the West into this whirlwind of consumer goods, media overkill, online buddies, bills, stress, and hyper-productivity. And it isn't limited to the environment. Our dreams, night and day, are riddled with clutter. We are constantly trying to juggle responsibilities, priorities, morality, ethics, memory, creativity, productivity, and spirituality in our minds. The worst part of this may be that we almost unconsciously and passively just seem to accept this assault. It took me a dramatic change, a move half a world and several cultures away, to open my eyes to the clutter of our way of life.

About twenty years ago my wife and I accepted teaching positions at the Daqing Petroleum Institute in northwestern China. The journey itself was to be a bewildering introduction to a frustrating slowing of the pace of our lives. On the twenty-two hour China Air flight, the Chinese flight attendants spent hours playing with our six-month-old son, unconcerned about the other passengers' immediate needs. Once in Beijing, we spent several days wandering through historical squares, palaces, and, of course, along the Great Wall that meanders so powerfully through the Chinese countryside. Finally, we boarded the train, one of China's many remaining steam engines, for the twenty-hour journey north to the city of Anda and the Institute where we were to teach English to bright young engineering students as well as to many grizzled old English teachers. For the next year our lives would slow down in dramatic fashion. Without television, restaurants and clubs, movies, or malls we had few distractions. We walked the mile to our classes each morning and afternoon, quickly at first, the way the typical Bisy Backson American walks. We were in a hurry, so much so that we would pass the Chinese as they rolled along slowly on their heavy black Seagull bicycles. When we'd get back to our own fifth-floor apartment, we didn't have a place to rush out to: no soccer practice, no shopping, no meeting for coffee, no having to get to the bank to pay a late bill. We were just there. We had one another, our little boy, a few books, our lessons and student papers, and the usual requirements of a day: eating, washing, going to the bathroom, sleeping—living. At first, we were bored and frequently frustrated. I think our American brains were moving much faster than our Chinese home. Then something happened. When we walked, we began to join our Chinese colleagues and students, slowly, unhurriedly. Our days began to seem plenty full. We talked, read, visited with our neighbors and students; we played with and cared for our child. And we wrote a great deal: letters, journals, stories, songs.

When, after a year in China, we returned to the United States, we were nearly overwhelmed by the intensity of American society, of the distraction, the cultural noise we westerners have created. I remember our first day back. Michael Jackson's "Thriller" video and album had just been released, the hotel elevator and lobby were wired for sound, the streets were fast and loud, television stations broadcast excess over hundreds of channels, and, worst of all, everyone was in a rush to get somewhere. After our year in the gentle pace of northwest China, we were overwhelmed and disoriented by the sudden onslaught of busy-ness. Sadly, reports from China suggest that the country has become increasingly westernized over the past twenty years, and Asian Bisy Backsons are on the rise. And, of course, we too have long since regained, and even surpassed, our former breakneck pace.

Our experience is not unusual. We know that newcomers to a place begin to take on the accent and mannerisms of the locals, and people who move to a quieter, more contemplative place begin to absorb that quiet. Writers often seek out quiet places and try to shed the hyper-clutter and distractions that characterize modern life. They seek a meditative place where they can begin to walk with the rhythms of another, less distracted state, the state of flow I describe earlier in the book. This is the Tao.

Arrangement: Room, Furniture, Walls, Doors, and Windows

The first rule of spatial arrangement is that it pleases. I can remember as a child occasionally arranging and rearranging my bedroom. I didn't do it often, and I don't recall whether or not my shifting followed any particular design, but even the small changes possible in my tiny room were satisfying.

The order of the writing space is significant. The orientation of the space, where the writer sits and works, the placement of the furniture and the directions of doors and windows, all of this is important to the writer's interaction with the space, the energy flow and the chi—for the writer's craft.

It begins with the entrance. The Chinese equated the entry of a building or room to the mouth. It had to be free of barriers, free of cutter. Ah, yes, we're back to clutter. It is important to keep the pathway to the door clear to ensure a free flow of positive energy into the space. This energy, positive *chi*, washes into the writing space, over the tools of the trade and the writer who uses them. It pays to be tidy.

In my own experience, I have changed my own orientation to the doorway in my office. I now face the open door, and the difference is remarkable. People passing by feel welcome and rarely hesitate to stop in and talk or to simply say hello. Others simply smile or wave as they pass the doorway. What's more, I feel far more productive than when I was facing the corner. Perhaps it is because I have room to breathe.

Once the energy flows in, like warm air, it seeks the high ground. This means that it isn't good to write in the basement or the root cellar. I've always been partial to a room with a view, the second floor overlooking my wooded back yard. Find a place that feels good and is located on the entry level or higher.

Points of Feng Shui for the Writer

Here are some points to consider as you attempt to create a writing space with the right energy and atmosphere for creativity.

Don't work in your bedroom

Feng shui experts warn against mixing bedroom sleep energies with work. If you have to work in your bedroom area, it's best to put up a screen between your work and sleeping spaces.

Choose a well-lighted place

Good chi requires life and that requires light. The writing space should have at least one window. If that isn't possible, paint the walls and ceiling a bright white or yellow and install a fan to get the positive energy flowing. Bright, pleasant pictures and posters will also bring in positive chi. When you choose a lamp, opt for the most natural artificial lighting you can find.

Don't hide in a corner

Place your desk or writing table with your back to a corner or wall. This creates a solid grounding, a secure place. Face the door if possible. If you must face the wall, your back to the door, place a mirror in front of you so you can see the door. In addition, if you have to sit facing a window with your back to the door, mirrors reflect the room behind you, offering solidity.

Get rid of it!

Clear away the junk. Removing unneeded and unwanted clutter makes room for new energy and new useful things. For ten years or more, I have had a small, two-cup coffee maker in my office, and I have made coffee with it no more than ten times in all those years—none in the past five years. In fact, I gave up drinking coffee two years ago. It is time to get rid of the little black coffee maker. Each person, no doubt, has dozens of such place keepers and space takers. All of this clutter is an enormous distraction, and as writers, we work best with the least distraction.

Calm the energies

A dark rug in the middle of the space—a deep blue is preferable—is said to be like a deep, restful, calming pool of water.

Commune with nature

Finally, try to situate your writing space so you can see the outside. If that isn't possible, hang a pastoral picture or a picture of a plant or the outdoors, and bring in live plants, placed where you can see them. Natural elements have a calming effect and can make for a more productive writing space.

Atmosphere: Color, Light, and Sound

The creative process seems to work the best in familiar, comfortable settings. This is no surprise to most of us. With some exceptions, we work best in an environment that is safe and warm, a place where we can let down our guard and open ourselves to intuition and inspiration. Of course, for most of us, this tends not to be a villa in the Alps, and it doesn't have to be. It is up to us to transform our own immediate environment in the way that enhances our own personal creativity. We all do this to some extent. We bring the right objects and furnishings into our homes and offices to make them comfortable on our own terms. As Mihaly Csikszentmihalyi says, "We need a supportive symbolic ecology in the home so that we can feel safe, drop our defenses, and go on with the tasks of life." He adds that these "essential traits and values of the self . . . help us be more unique, more creative" (142).

The writer's environment should reflect his or her creative needs and tastes. The atmosphere should enhance the creative process. This includes the colors, sounds, and even the light that we invite into a space. For example, I am currently at my kitchen table. It is late November and the wind is driving in hard from the East, bringing with it, I'm told, three to six inches of snow. Outside, the thermometer reads thirty degrees Fahrenheit, yet the grass is a deep green under the towering pines and the old, leafless maple beyond. The sky is a foreboding gray. Inside, the teapot simmers on low, ready to keep my cup filled. The lighting is warm but bright, and an old, stained kitchen radio plays morning jazz from a Toronto station. Although it's nearly nine o'clock, most of my family is still asleep, taking advantage of Saturday. This is when I am at my best and most productive. Each of us must find or create this writer's atmosphere for ourselves.

Color

Color holds a significant place in the Taoist cosmology. This is no great surprise as color has meaning beyond simple shades and tones in all cultures. It has a particularly important role in literature: The play of light and dark, black and white in *The Strange Case of Doctor Jekyll and Mister Hyde,* the stifling pale atmosphere in Camus' *The Stranger.* The symbolic use of color is profoundly significant in our stories, mythology, religion, and ritual. I once heard an author say that all her favorite stories begin with color. I wanted to know if it was true, so I glanced at a few of the books on my shelf. Jack London's *White Fang* begins with a scene in a forest, "black and ominous in the fading light," and one of my all-time favorite novels, John Kennedy Toole's *A Confederacy of Dunces*, opens with, "A green hunting cap squeezed the top of the fleshy balloon of a head." Toole adds green earflaps, a bushy black moustache, and yellow eyes in the first paragraph. John Steinbeck's *The Grapes of Wrath* begins, "To the red country and part of the gray country of Oklahoma, the last rains came gently, and they did not cut the scarred earth."

Another remarkable novel opens with a rich splash of color and suggestion of color: Arundhati Roy's *The God of Small Things* begins, "May in Ayemenem is a hot, brooding month. The days are long and humid. The river shrinks and black crows gorge on bright mangoes in still, dustgreen trees. Red bananas ripen. Dissolute bluebottles hum vacuously in the fruity air. Then they stun themselves against clear windowpanes and die, fatly baffled in the sun."

It is true that some books and short stories like the ones above do indeed begin with color, but at least on my shelves, most don't. I was disappointed because my instinct, my deep memory of stories, told me that the statement rang true. Then it dawned on me. Words come to us in shades, a palette of colors, even when no color is actually mentioned. We sense color in moods, so why wouldn't we sense red, green, or blackness in the words we read and, of course, the words we write? Consider W. W. Jacob's classic short story, "The Monkey's Paw." It's a tale that illustrates in graphic terms the saying, "Be careful what you wish for." The story begins, "Without, the night was cold and wet, but in the small parlour of Laburnum Villa the blinds were drawn and the fire burned brightly." No color is mentioned, but we can feel the cold, wet, deep blue of the night, and the warm golden fire and earth tones of the parlour. *Jane Eyre* begins, "There was no possibility of taking a walk that day. We had been wandering, indeed, in the leafless shrubbery an hour in the morning; but since dinner . . . the cold winter wind had brought with it clouds so somber, and a rain so penetrating, that further outdoor exercise was out of the question." Here, Charlotte Bronte paints a landscape of gray tones and gloom, setting the tone for the tale to come.

The colors of our world create and affect our moods. This is undeniable. We use color to decorate, to manipulate our inner and outer spaces. In the most extreme examples, people experience aspects of the world such as taste, music, or even the words on the page as intense color. This neurological condition, known as synesthesia, is almost a literal realization of common sayings: I'm seeing red; she's green with envy; he's yellow; I'm feeling a little blue; she's in a black mood; and so on. Although, color does not affect most of us so dramatically or obviously, it affects us all in surprisingly powerful ways. This is the reason we rarely find a room that is entirely black, deep red, or other dark color. We're more likely to live in spaces painted in light colors, off-whites, tans, pastels. Dark colors carry certain connotations and have physical qualities that affect us in clear ways. Dark colors absorb light, often making it hard to light our inner spaces. Specific colors seem to affect people in predictable ways. For instance, blues are quiet, cool, and wet. Too much can create an unsettling, sterile coolness, but in the right setting and the right amount, blue can be quiet and meditative. Strong reds and oranges are exciting, sometimes invigorating, sometimes enervating.

The Taoist, or feng shui, view of various colors follows (adapted from Richard Webster's *101 Feng Shui Tips*):

- Red—When we think of the color red, we think of fire, anger, excitement, and blood. It can be the color of happiness, passion, and prosperity, or it can create nervousness and tension in our lives. It can lead to our seeing red. Be careful to balance red with calmer, softer colors.
- Orange—A motivated, sociable, earth element. The passion of red is softened by yellow creating a good-natured feeling. Orange is a good choice for study areas.
- Yellow—What could be happier than a bright yellow? Yellow is the color of the sun, of dandelions and buttercups. It brings to mind a cheerful summer's day, laughter, and warmth.
- Green—Green is the color of the forest, alive in spring, the color of renewal. It is the color of new buds, rebirth, and nature itself.
- Blue—Blue is the cool of water, the innate spirituality and magic of twilight, and the meditative tranquility of the sky or a calm sea.
- Violet—The magician wears violet, a color of mystery and magic, the color of mysticism and wonder.
- Gold—Gold color shines like its precious metal namesake, like fame, like dignity. Gold is the color of luck.
- White—White brings to mind purity and innocence, goodness, clarity of purpose, a bright, open place.
- Black—In the West, we often see black as ominous and evil, but in feng shui black can be powerful, a bringer of riches, especially used with white and other colors and used sparingly.

If the idea of enhancing your writing through color appeals and you wish to look into it more thoroughly, consider Richard Webster's book *101 Feng Shui Tips*, and the others listed at the end of this book. Remember, color is part of us and affects how we feel and perform in a space. We can energize our writing areas using bright colors or create a place of meditation and inspiration using cooler colors. No one color is perfect for anyone. Try mixing tones. Ultimately, color can be a wonderful asset to the writer's flow.

Light

"Remember the clear light, the pure clear white light from which everything in the universe comes, to which everything in the universe returns; the original nature of your own mind; the natural state of the universe unmanifest. Let go into the clear light, trust it, merge with it. It is your own true nature, it is home" (Teachings of the Buddha—from The Tibetan Book of the Dead).

The Tao Te Ching tells us, "It is by shielding intellect's bright light that the sage remains at one with his own self, ceasing to be aware of it, by placing it behind" (verse 7). The light of the Tao is essential, but it remains in the background, supporting and giving vitality and inspiration to our endeavors and our spaces.

We can energize our living and working spaces with light. Sunlight gives us energy and a sense of well-being. Garish artificial light, such as the kind of white fluorescent lights that used to be common in office buildings and is still a staple in garages, basements, and workshops, can over-stimulate, nerve us up. Soft, natural light has a warm, comforting quality. In feng shui, light can energize our productivity, luck, and harmony if it is used properly. If used improperly, it can energize the negative aspects of our lives, creating disharmony and loss.

Your writing space should be well lighted in the most natural way possible. The best light comes from a generally northern exposure. The pure light that filters through a north-facing window is the light of the artist—the most balanced, diffuse light. Artificial lighting must be both warm and bright enough to write by comfortably, without eyestrain or excessive glare. In feng shui, the ways we interact with lighting is practical but, in its most detailed form, is highly involved. For more on light and the Tao, explore Lillian Too's works on feng shui and spaces.

Sound

I confess that I nearly omitted this part of the book. When I began thinking about atmosphere, color, and light, sound came to mind, but I was having trouble finding information about the connections between the Tao and sound. I was looking too hard; I was looking in the wrong places. First and last the Tao is inside of us.

The sound of the Tao is in the eternal cycle of breathing. It is the whisper of a light breeze and the howl of fierce winds, the breath of the world. It is in the beating of hearts, the growling of stomachs, the crying and laughing of babies and all humanity, in murmurs of pleasure, moans of pain—in essence, the sound of the Tao is the hum of the universe, the world, and of our place in it, including our writing spaces.

Just as the colors and light around us affect how and what we write, so does what we hear through our ears, our bodies and our souls, through our skin and bones, through our very cells. As I said, I was looking too hard. The answer was right there in my writing space. Although I often listen to public radio in the mornings, I can't write well and can't think clearly with the banter of radio hosts in the background. I thrive on the relative silence of my house, the morning sounds of the house settling, the teapot heating, the birds and squirrels in the yard, the steady mantra of a morning rain, the thunder of a passing storm, or the soft silence of a new snowfall. At times I'll listen to music, soft jazz, blues, or the meditative beauty of baroque music. I'm not alone. Research on the effects of sound on our moods and temperament show clear ties between what we hear and how we feel and, of course, what we do. Just as the clutter of paper and obsolete artifacts distracts us, so does the clutter of sound. Talk radio, the news of the day, entertaining conversation all draw our attention away from the muse inside. Of course, it can be fine to share our proofreading or editing time, the more mechanical parts of writing, with radio and television personalities, but for the creative moment, sound clutter will block the flow so necessary to most writers.

Sound is everywhere. It permeates our outer and inner spaces every moment of every day. The other night I heard someone say that he'd bought earplugs to help him sleep and was surprised to discover just how loud the inside of his head was. Sound can be healing as with ultralow-frequency treatment or music therapy, or it can be destructive in the way low- and high-frequency vibrations can shake a building apart or shatter a pane of glass. In the Tao, as in many great philosophies of history, the awareness of our aural universe can help us on the path to higher awareness. Chants, songs, and mantras are evident in every culture and every metaphysical and spiritual path. The famous Gregorian Chant of the Catholic Church bears a remarkable resemblance to the meditative mantras of Hindi adepts and Buddhist monks. Native American and African tribal rhythmic chanting, Christian prayer, and Gospel music bring both a common experience and a personal connection to the universe, to the Creator. The chanting practice literally allows us to become attuned to the universe.

For the creative space, sound enhances or detracts from flow. Of course, each of us is different, having different tastes in music and such, but here are some guidelines for using sound to your advantage.

Begin the writing session with a moment of meditation. This might include the quiet of an early morning and cup of tea, or you may choose to consciously meditate. In either case, the sounds of your surroundings should be quiet and centering. Begin your writing session in this soft tunnel of sound, wrapped in the subtlety of the natural world, gentle New Age melodies, or a Vivaldi concerto. If it fits your mood and the writing task, you might choose to do most of your writing while inside this deeply contemplative, meditative environment. Many of us, however, will shift to a more energetic atmosphere—maybe jazz, Celtic music, or blues—later in the day. In the end, we each must do what works for us. Like the avant-garde painter who creates in the maelstrom of blaring punk music, rock and roll, a particular writer or writing task may take form in an atmosphere of chaos and hyper energy. The important thing is that we tap into the power of our environment using it to bring us closer to the source, to tie us into the flow of the Tao.

The Writer's Tools

"When wood is shaped, it becomes tools.
Used by the sage, tools become powerful."

(Tao Te Ching, verse 28)

Personal Preferences

Just as the place is important to writing well, so are the writer's tools. Mark Twain is said to have preferred to draft on long sheets of blue paper using purple ink. Edmund White tells us, "I write in longhand, and I write in very beautiful notebooks and with very beautiful pens" (Krementz, 108). William Styron has said that his preference is to write with number two pencils and yellow legal pads. Personally, I write most comfortably with a slim fountain or roller-ball pen in dark black ink on the pages of the old style black-and-white composition notebooks. Why do I and others care so much about the tools we write with? In my own case, I like the way certain pens feel in my hand. I like the flow of jet black India ink and the sensation of a smooth fountain pen nib on a clean page. A good roller-ball pen is my second choice because of availability and cost. I can't tell you why I enjoy writing with certain tools, but I know that, like me, most writers tend to have distinct preferences for certain shapes and colors of writing tools.

Practicing What I Preach

I know firsthand the problems associated with a cluttered writing space. I am infamous for piles of papers, disorganized file cabinets, stacks of books and magazines, much of which I've never actually read and probably never will, and memo sheets pasted, taped, and stapled across just about any flat surface. My offices have always been a mess. This is extremely bad, or shar chi, in feng shui terms. I can't argue with the need to create order in this disorder. I have never been able to work very effectively in my office, as it has always become a negative space under the piles of useless paper and the constant traffic, so I hid. I actually found I could write better just about anywhere but at the desk in my office. I found I could write at the shop while my car was being serviced (a little oily smelling, but quiet, pleasant, and coffee and tea were complimentary); in the bathroom (comfortable, familiar, and there is little chance of interruption); in my car while waiting for my daughter to get out of orchestra practice, gymnastics, choir, etc. (all familiar, warm, and relatively uncluttered spaces); and even in a back corner of the library (isolated, quiet, devoid of clutter and distraction). The irony here, of course, is that my office should be all of this: quiet, uncluttered, warm, familiar, and comfortable. It just has never been.

On top of the mess, my office arrangement was physically uncomfortable, inconvenient, and counter to common sense and good chi (the flow of energy in a space). When using my computer, I faced east, looking out the window over the asphalt parking lot. My back was to the door, my face lost in a computer monitor, and around me was a chaos of paper and machinery— very shar chi. Not only was I leaving my back unprotected, in feng shui terms, but the clutter was a physical wall to those

162

wanting to see me, and my back-to-the-door position was clearly a psychological barrier.

So I began the transformation. I was somewhat limited by my furniture and the arrangement of electrical outlets, computer connections, and such, but I set out to make my space better for me, my students, and the office in general.

First, I began to shovel out the piles of paper, old files, and books. My usual problem with shoveling out is that I manage to get part of the way into the job, and the piles begin to grow again. I don't expect that every cluttering habit will disappear, so I'm willing to live with some of the mess, but I am determined to keep the piles at bay, at least below chest level.

Next, in order to begin rearranging my workplace, I established a set of objectives:

1. I want to create a space that lends itself more naturally to order;
2. I want to create a space that is pleasant to be in;
3. I want to create a space that is conducive to reading and writing;
4. I want to create a space that welcomes visitors;
5. I want to create a space that brings people together, a comfortable, welcoming meeting place; and
6. I want to create a space where positive energy (hau chi) can flow freely.

Consider your own writing (and living) space. How well does it accomplish the goals of the above list? Think of the ways you could change your space and your habits to create a more productive writing space.

A Final Word

We have been deceived. In fact, we have expended a great deal of personal energy on deceiving ourselves, on convincing ourselves that writing is too hard, too painful, and we've decided that the best solution is to avoid writing as often as possible. Most of us have come to think of writing as something other people do (or do not do) well, as a mysterious, unnatural process which is open to a select few. As a result, we seem to want to separate ourselves from writing, as if it is a chair on the far side of the room, or to run away from it, reject it, because we've learned that writing is a kind of punishment. The Tao shows us that we are all connected to the power of writing, that it is not the property of an elite few, and that it is as natural to us as breathing. The Tao shows us that writing is a great gift, that it is part of the flow, of everything. The Tao shows us that we have inside each of us the power to make written language our own, to drain the energy from the negative messengers. We've learned that writing is part of the flow of the Tao, of everything. Everything in life is essential to the journey, to the Tao. We tend to put our lives in little boxes, compartments holding pieces of our existence. Our jobs are separate from family life, which is separate from our recreation and entertainment, which is separate from our spiritual worlds, and so on. The truth is there are no compartments. It is all interconnected, blended in the flow of the Tao. The words we write weave in and through this beautiful, relentless current, adding their influence to the chi of the universe. In this, we have little choice. Who we are and what we do are of the Tao. It is inevitable. We can, however, choose how we wish to participate, to make that journey. The Tao does not play favorites. Its great universal river carries everything and everyone equally, without hesitation. In it are rocks, log jams, swirling eddies. In writing, as in all human endeavors, we seem to hunt for the rocks, aim for the logjams, and twirl about in the eddies, confused and distracted. The Tao asks only that we open ourselves, our writing, to the natural flow of the universe, to choose the Tao of writing and, indeed, of living.

Part 4

Writing Activities

It isn't difficult to find writing activities that play on Taoist philosophy. Writing is a creative endeavor, and creative people tend to search for ways of allowing their creativity to flow. The following activities can help to set your writing in motion and establish a momentum that can continue almost effortlessly. (Note: I've included in this section some versions of a few of the exercises found earlier in the book; this way all of the suggested exercises can be found in one place.) Remember, these are not formal writing assignments. Interpret and approach them freely.

Enjoy them.

1. Visualization

Relax and take your time with this meditative exercise. Create a character in your mind's eye. See the character's features, colors, build, clothes, gestures, and way of moving. Hear the character's voice. Visualize the setting, action, and details surrounding the character. When you have explored the character fully, free write about the experience.

2. The River

You are a river flowing through space and time. You pass places, people, events (anything you wish). Quickly jot down as many of these as you can. First, list the events and such that you pass as you flow along in this cosmic river. This is important, and anything goes here. Then, in five to ten minutes for each, write down your series of vignettes.

3. The Wheel

Exercise A: Just as the solid parts of the bicycle or wagon wheel (the hub; the spokes) can be compared to the main characters of a story, the spaces between these solid parts can be the background, the often subtle details that fill in behind and around the main action. Choose a short story, novel, or essay and write several pages in which you describe the background events and details that allow the main characters and actions to exist.

Exercise B: Write a story using only supporting characters and background events and details. The main character, conflict, and action should be implied, not stated.

4. Wu Wei (writing without writing)

Put your pen and paper away. Find a voice recorder and, in a quiet place where you won't be disturbed or feel self-conscious, talk about your essay, story, proposal, or whatever writing task you've set for yourself. Record this monologue. Speak freely without concern for structure or correctness. Talk it out. Talk it over. Talk it through. Later you may wish to go back to listen for ideas, to transcribe part or all of what you've said, or you may simply set it aside and begin writing.

5. The Tree

Choose a topic. This can be a story idea, a character, setting or situation, or a topic for an essay, proposal, or whatever suits you. Write down the ten most important points you can think of about the topic. If you're pressed for time, write four. Now write each at the top of a separate piece of paper. Beginning with the first, free write on that point for ten to fifteen minutes. Do the same for point two, point three, and so on. When you've done all ten (this may be over two or three sittings) arrange the papers in order. You will probably have fifteen to thirty pages and, most likely, a good start on your manuscript.

6. The Journey

Take a character on a journey. Establish a starting point and a destination. Then tell the story of that journey. Place three complications, impediments, or problems along the way. Write through these problems (people, events, etc.) until the character reaches the destination.

7. Anticipation

Free write on your deepest desire. Then write a scene in which you approach achieving that profound desire. Remember, the key is to write the approach, the buildup, not the moment, as Pooh would say, of finally tasting the honey.

8. Breathing

Quietly observe your breath for a long moment—five to twenty minutes, depending on your level of concentration. Then write a detailed description of breathing, a complete sensory description of the passage of air in and out of your body. Describe only one cycle of inhaling and exhaling: the sensations of taste, smell, movement, temperature, sound, interaction with other parts of the body, etc.

9. The Mountain

Write with the voice of the mountain: quiet, powerful, enduring, seemingly immobile, yet ever-changing.

10. Listening

Close your eyes and meditate quietly for five to ten minutes. Focus on sounds. Listen with full attention. Only listen. What do you hear? Write for fifteen minutes on the experience.

11. Beads

All great religions and philosophies use beads in their contemplative practice. Catholics use the Rosary, Buddhists their prayer beads, Muslims the mesbah, and Bahai the Subha. Tie ten knots about two inches apart on a length of cord. For each knot write a brief story or scene that leads to the next and emerges from the last. If you tie the two ends of the cord together, you may continue this exercise almost endlessly.

12. Forgiveness

Exercise A: Imagine a character who is unable to forgive a slight or insult. Write about what happens to this character.
Exercise B: Write this same character finding forgiveness.

13. The Pond

I once lived near a small neighborhood pond. On the surface it seemed placid and, except for the occasional frog or turtle and a few lily pads, fairly uninteresting. When I looked more closely, however, I saw that it was teeming with creatures: small fish and minnows, pollywogs, turtles, snakes, and countless varieties of insects and tiny forms of water life and plants. Birds and other animals would drink and hunt at the pond. It was not overly deep, but it was remarkably rich.

Imagine a tranquil pond. Then, slowly, visualize what you find as you look deeper and deeper into the waters. Write as vivid a description as possible of this dramatic world. Consider writing this pond narrative from several perspectives: the outside observer, a creature living in the pond, even the pond itself.

14. The Wind

The wind moves where it wishes. Your narrator is the wind drifting or howling through places, lives, events, touching each momentarily. Write a narrative from the wind's point of view that describes these brief encounters.

15. Internal Talk

Writers waste time and energy with negative mind-chatter. Reject the negative messages you give yourself (I can't write, I hate writing, It's too much, I'll never be any good at this) and create a new set of positive messages for yourself (I'm a good writer, I have something important to say, I love writing, Writing gives me power, I can create worlds with my writing).

16. Discovery

Close your eyes and relax. Now imagine yourself walking down a pleasant hallway, city street, or country path. On either side of you are doors or gates. Choose one and open it slowly. Describe what you discover on the other side. What does the place look like? Who or what inhabits that place. Go to another portal and do the same. Narrate what you find in writing.

17. The Circle

This is an old group exercise that can be a lot of fun, but it also highlights the flowing nature of writing.

Writers sit in a circle. Each is given a prompt on a piece of paper (it may be the same prompt, or each person might have a unique story starter). It might be "Karl stood rock still, hoping the gigantic being would overlook him" or "They had been in the apartment for nearly fifteen minutes before Natalie noticed the open window" or something the writers created. Each writer writes the next line in this potential story and passes it to the person on the right. This person adds the next line, and so on.

This exercise can go on until the writers choose to end their stories, or each can be given an assigned task: Writer #1 introduces a main character and a setting; Writer #2 establishes conflict; Writer #3 brings in a minor character and a dialogue exchange; Writer #4 resolves the conflict for the moment; Writer #5 complicates the situation; Writer #6 brings the story line to a climax; Writer #7 resolves the story.

18. Flow

Coherent writing is like a waterfall, the wind, a river, and the cycle of life. Just as each part of our lives, our experiences, our breathing, our moment to moment changes and growth, all of this demonstrates the flow inherent in the Tao. This series of exercises can help writers understand and use this coherence in their work.

This is best done with two or more writers, but an individual can try it as well.

Write a short passage based on a prompt. It could be "I believe . . .," "I've never told this to anyone . . ." or another of your choosing. It matters little, as long as it gets the writer writing. Then the writer passes the paragraph to a second writer who begins the second passage with the last word of the first. The writer must also use two or three important words from the passage. These will appear in the first sentence of the new paragraph. Continue like this until the paper has been passed on at least six times.

19. Change

The permanence of the world is illusory. As the Tao tells us, nothing is static. Sit and observe a place for an hour, an afternoon, or a day. Jot down the changes you see from moment to moment: the shifts of light, temperature, mood; the comings and goings of people, animals, insects, clouds, shadow. Note the changes in sand, dust, and color. You may even take your observations to the microscopic, invisible worlds and describe the subtle changes you sense or imagine. Taoism acknowledges that the world is constantly in flux, always moving and changing like the river and the wind. Learn to notice and celebrate this change.

20. Changing Stories

Rewrite part (or all) of a favorite story or poem. Change it as you like. Make the character different; make the villain more villainous. Change the ending. Do whatever you like. This exercise can be great fun with your favorite classic fairy tales.

21. Singing the Story

I once gave an academic lecture entirely in song at a national conference. Find something you've written in prose—perhaps a short story, an essay, a letter to a friend, or even your resume—and rewrite it as a song or poem. First, outline the main sections and topics of the piece. Then, turn each of these into a verse or stanza.

22. Seeing Personal Change

This is an exercise in creative visualization. In the 1980s, I was enthralled by Shakti Gawain's book *Creative Visualization*. I discovered it was a powerful way to motivate myself and, thus, change my world. Writing increases that power significantly.

Get comfortable, and have pen and paper ready. Think about something in your life that you would like to change. It might be related to your love life, politics, living situation, job—anything that is important to you. Imagine it changed. Imagine everything as you hope it to be once the change has taken place. Begin to write about the situation or condition you wish to change. What is it? Why should it change? Now write a story in which the change happens. Include yourself as the main character in the narrative about change. What does your character do to create change? What outside forces come into play?

23. Changing the World

Write the world anew. Find a situation or practice that troubles or annoys you. Rewrite that piece of the world. Most writers will want to create an ideal. Experiment with less-than-perfect alternatives; play with the darker aspects of the world if you wish.

24. Remake the Predictable

Create a song, a poem, or a story from a mundane, real-life work document: a shopping or grocery list, a presentation, study notes. In graduate school I wrote a song I called "Damned Foucault" that presented a sketch of my doctoral reading list. It was a way to help me deal with the stress of my upcoming exams, but it also turned out to be a helpful study aid, and pretty entertaining to boot.

Try something similar with your own writing. Play with the form. Create something completely off the wall and unpredictable from the most commonplace. Enjoy this one.

25. Unity

Find a face in a crowd, on the street, passing you in the hall, or sitting across from you in a restaurant. It is the face of somebody you don't know. Discreetly observe the expression, skin tone and texture, angle of the mouth, shape of the chin and nose, and the color, cut, and fall of the hair. Pay particular attention to the eyes in this face, their shape, color, and depth. Now create a name, something that expresses who this person is, or more accurately, who this character might be. Jot down the details of this person's life: height, weight, features, skin, eye and hair colors, home town, education, parents, brothers and sisters, job, ethnicity, hobbies, relationships, beliefs, desires, motivations, fears, strengths, flaws or weaknesses, pets, clothing style, habits, and movements.

26. Multiplying Tree

This is a looping exercise described by Peter Elbow in *Writing with Power* and later, in this form, by my friend Susan Leist.

Free write on a tough problem or concern for twenty to thirty minutes (less if you're new to free writing). The topic could be a difficulty at work, an impasse in a piece of writing, a personal problem—it's up to you. When you've completed the free write, read through it and circle one or more lines or passages that strike you as significant. It may be something that hints at a solution or begins to look at the problem from an entirely new, unexpected perspective.

Then, beginning with a significant line, free write for twenty to thirty minutes. Repeat this process. Do this exercise over a number of days, allowing yourself the time and space to percolate between writings. The results are surprising.

27. Touching the Universe

Chinese Taoists send messages and gifts of paper money into the universe by burning slips of paper and "lay money" during Chinese New Year. This exercise is very simple. Copy out some of your favorite passages, poems, stories, lines from your own writing, and such. You may want to write new bits especially for this activity. Then, on a small, safe fire or in the fireplace, ignite these words letting them drift into the sky and beyond. This is the manifestation of letting go and a concrete offering to the universe.

28. The Sanctuary

This is a variation on a popular "New Age" meditation/visualization exercise from the 1970s.

Relax. Close your eyes and get comfortable, but not so comfortable that you fall asleep. You might begin with a breathing meditation or muscle relaxation. Have paper and pen at hand.

Now, imagine you are in a wonderful place. It might be a beautiful beach setting, a lovely meadow, or anything that makes you happy. In my own case, I enjoy visualizing a cold November scene on a rocky coast. Weird? Maybe, but it ties me to some happy times, and, in spite of the icy illusion, it makes me feel warm, safe, and at peace.

Once you're in your own place, begin to explore. What do you see, feel, smell, taste, hear? Then, create whatever you wish in your place. Would you like to see dolphins, unicorns, or creatures from your own imagination? Are people there? Would you like to create a cabin, mansion, castle? You can do whatever you wish because this is your visualization.

When you have explored and created to your heart's content, open your eyes, pick up your pen, and write a description of the experience. Include all the sensory details and impressions.

29. Clarity

Exercise A: Choose a passage from a favorite (or not so favorite) piece of writing and rewrite it, paring it down to its essential bones. See how few words you can use without losing the meaning and tone of the passage.
Exercise B: Choose one of your favorite passages from your own writing and rewrite it, boiling it down to its essence. Use as few words as you can manage. Try to retain its original meaning and tone.

30. Beyond Clarity

Write a scene in which the narrator can hear other people's thoughts. How does the character react? What does such hyperclarity reveal about the people the character thinks he or she knows?

31. Seeing Again

Re-read a piece you've been working on. Set it aside, and pick up a sketchpad. Draw images that reflect the themes in the writing—what the writing says and means. This is not an art assignment, and you need not be a skilled artist. Your drawings (you can use any medium you like) are simply representations of ideas, feelings, concepts, and they do not have to look a certain way. There is no wrong way to represent your work. Interpreting words through image and color, even sculpture if you wish, adds dimension to text and literally allows us to revise, to see again, what we have written.

32. Snap a Picture

The next time you find yourself in the presence of inspiration, snap a picture in words. It could be a moment when a piece of music fills you, or as you watch a loved one sleeping, dancing, or just being; it might be at the summit of a mountain, in the glow of a glorious sunset or meteor shower, or as you feel the warmth of grains of sand against your skin. There is no rule for what inspires you. Stop a moment, take out your pen and paper, and write for five or ten minutes. Fill the page with images, sounds, and sensations. Don't be surprised if ten minutes turns into an hour.

33. Touching Nature

You are just as natural as a wolf, a tree, a slug, or the bit of fungus that grows on your shower wall. Write a short piece in which you meld with an aspect of what you consider to be the natural world. For example, become the face of a rugged cliff, or a mosquito coming in for (or becoming) a meal. Take on the voice of this natural entity. Tell your history and your view of humanity, specifically of the writer (you).

34. The Animal Nature

Describe yourself as an animal. Which animal might it be? What characteristics would you highlight? Then try another animal.

35. The Eye of a Hurricane

Imagine you are a great natural event such as a magnificent thunderstorm, a hurricane, a blizzard, a tornado, or an earthquake. Write the experience of being nature at its most powerful, destructive, even beautiful. You might use words and images that evoke this power, movement, and energy, or you might choose to explore the more sublime, philosophical character of the event.

36. Place

Human beings have a strong sense of place, in spite of our recent attempts to ignore it. We come from and identify strongly with a place, a landscape, a people and their culture. For example, my best fiction seems to bring me back to the Upper Peninsula of Michigan, the woods, the sound of the locals, the cool or bitterly cold weather and snow, and the great icy Lake Superior. I write about it, I suppose, because it lives in my memory, and I feel it in my bones. Meditate on your place, your geographical and sentimental roots, and write a letter to a distant friend describing the place, the people, the light, the innate sense of connection you feel. Create a story set in this place.

37. Dear Diary

Keep a diary of personal feelings. We tend to think of this as something only teenagers, usually girls, do. Go ahead. It is fun to put our deepest thoughts and desires in writing, and it can be both meditative and therapeutic.

38. Creation

We are all familiar with the Creation Story as told in the Bible. Many may be familiar with similar stories from American Indian, African, and other cultures as well. Write your own story of creation beginning with . . . you tell me.

39. The Universe

Find a hollow egg. One of the plastic Easter eggs we find in many stores around the holiday will do, or, if you happen to have a Fabergé egg on the bookshelf, that will do nicely as well. Put the hollow egg on the floor or table in front of you. Clear away all distractions. You will need to focus your attention entirely upon the egg. Now, imagine a world or a universe existing inside the egg. Describe this place in as much detail as you can. What would happen if you were to break the shell, to open the egg? Write a scene or a poem based on this exercise.

40. The Journey

The journey of the spirit has been a topic of literature, music, and art for as long as creative humanity has existed. All spiritual texts, the Bhavaghad Gita, the Koran, the Bible, and the Tao Te Ching, are literary manifestations of this remarkable journey.

In popular literature, the metaphor of the spiritual journey is expressed in Herman Hesse's work, notably *Siddhartha*, Castaneda's mystical adventures in the American southwest, C. S. Lewis' *Chronicles of Narnia*, and many, many more.

What symbolizes your own spiritual journey? Visualize a spiritual goal and the path or paths to getting there. Do a twenty-minute free write in which you explore this universal metaphor. It could be in clearly Taoist forms: the river, the wind, or a flower. It may take some other form altogether: an alien landscape, Eastern (oriental) philosophy, or a decidedly modern or postmodern vision as with William Gibson's *Neuromancer* or the recent film, *The Matrix*. What is your Taoist or spiritual journey?

41. Write a Meditation

What is the most meditative aspect of your life? Is it traditional sitting meditation, walking meditation, or conscious breathing? Is it religious prayer or reflection? Free write on what meditation means to you. Then draft a guide to your meditation. Make it informal and talky, as if you were helping a friend learn it. Add images, sketches, colors if you like. Record it and share the meditation with a loved one.

42. Peace Poem

Write the word—P E A C E—vertically on a page. Then write a word or line of words on peace beginning with each letter. This diacrostic poem can begin with any word or words you wish. Here is an example:

P ut away weapons and hatred
E nvelope all men and women in love
A llow the Tao to enter each heart
C limb the mountain of humility
E nter into peace

43. The Intentional Writer

The Tao is intentional. The writer slips into the natural flow through becoming involved in the world. Here are several ways in which a writer can harness the energy of the Tao.

Write a letter to a local official, politician, or newspaper pointing out a concern and advocating for change—environmental cleanup, health care, after-school programs—whatever issue is your passion.

Build a poetry wall at home, at work, at school, at the local library. Post poems. Encourage others to post poems that reflect the spirit of the Tao.

Join a writing group. You'll have fun, and nothing is better for a writer's craft than other writers.

44. Color

Some of the most striking and beautiful writing is immersed in color. Many stories and novels are memorable for their rich, deeply sensory colors; for example, Camus' *The Plague* and its deathly mundane yellow landscape, and Luis Arturo Ramos' hauntingly blue short story, "Underwater." Then, of course, Oz has its Emerald City, symbolizing promise and plenty. Color creates a visceral reaction in each of us, and it holds great meaning in the Taoist tradition. Try this:

- Write a poem in which a color is the primary metaphor. Try this with several colors, and see the difference.
- Write a short descriptive piece on a place and the overriding impressions of color there. Do this in first-person narrative. Then do it in third-person narrative.
- Write a short story in which the narrator sees the world through a color. What kind of world, conflict, action takes place through this tinted lens? What does the color tell us about the character? What happens when the color changes?

45. Seeing Color

You've heard the color clichés: to see red, in a blue mood, green-eyed monster or green with envy, he's yellow, in a black place, purple passion, and so on. Write a scene in which you exploit color to reflect the meaning of the phrase as thoroughly as possible:

To see red—Use the color red in a variety of ways to write/paint a scene, a mood, an action, and a character. You may follow the traditional meaning, to become angry, but change it up as well. Interpret red in your own way. Color the world red with imagery. Create a mood and energy with words that bring to life the essence of red.

Do the same with blue, green, brown, opal . . .

46. Being Inside Color

This is an exercise in feeling the colors around you. Find a room, a peaceful place in a park or woods, or a public place in which one color or tone predominates. For example, you may be in a small clearing in the woods surrounded and covered by lush greenery, or a dark meditative chapel, or a brightly painted children's room. Seek out different places, those that are rich with color or those that seem to lack color almost entirely. Write about the colors, the play of light, and the mood. Let the colors come into and flow through your body. Write freely in any form you wish. Do this in several color settings. What do you discover about color?

47. Peace Meditation

What do we mean when we talk about peace? Is it the absence of war? This a common definition in public policy and in the press. Or is it something more personal, more directly connected to each of us? We know that countries not engaged in war can be violent. Even generally peaceful places have their share of angry, violent events. So, what is peace? This meditation can help each of us find the answer to that question for ourselves.

Take a few moments to relax. Sit comfortably with pen and paper on a table, clipboard, or in a notebook in front of you. If you are very comfortable with a computer keyboard, you might choose to write electronically. In any case, be sure to use writing tools you like. Now close your eyes partially, softly, so you are focusing on nothing in particular. Begin to breathe slowly, consciously. Bring your awareness to your breathing. Silently say I am breathing in; I am breathing out. Do this until you feel calm and centered.

Now that you're relaxed, in your mind, go to a place, real or imagined, where you feel at peace. Notice your surroundings. Notice what makes this an especially peaceful place for you. Take it all in and enjoy the peacefulness.

Now begin to write. What have you discovered about peace? What can you do to bring the peace of this place into more of your life?

48. The Peace Journal

Writing can lead us to awareness. It is a way to discover and make knowledge and, most important, to learn more about who we are.

This activity will ground the writer in the idea and practice of peace-making in two important ways: first, it fosters awareness of what we do and don't do for peace each day; and second, it creates energy and a powerful impetus to take an active role in creating a peaceful place. It's important that this journal is kept regularly and that it focuses on peace.

In the evening, take a quiet moment to reflect on your day. When have you felt the most at peace in your day? What was the environment like? What about this experience felt peaceful? Were other people involved—did the peace extend to them as well? Next, consider what you have done during the day to create a better, more peaceful world. It need not be showy or profound. It could be a simple act: a smile for a stranger, a kind word, a kiss for a loved one; or it could be something grander or more political such as signing or distributing a petition, marching for peace, or writing letters to politicians or newspapers.

Finally, briefly reflect on what you might do tomorrow. How will you act to make the world better, more peaceful, who will be affected, and how might the world change with your act?

Keep this journal daily.

49. Hope

The great literature of history often reflects and symbolizes hope in a world that can seem hopeless. What does hope mean to you? What symbols represent hope to you? Write about hopeful symbols and the actions they represent. You may want to sketch the symbols as you write about them.

50. Affirmation Journal

Keep a daily journal of affirmations. We are inundated with negative images, and we may internalize this kind of destructive self-talk. Affirmations are just the opposite—positive, uplifting, motivating self-talk. We know that words have power and that the first step in achieving a goal can be to write it down, so it is important that we learn to wash over the negative messages with positive affirmations. These may be short, simple reminders to ourselves: I am a strong, happy individual; I'm a loving person; I am making the world a little bit better place; I am a successful writer, dancer, etc. These need not be complicated or grand. It doesn't take much to alter your outlook on life. In your journal try writing extended passages in which you detail the strengths and dreams you wish to affirm. For example, if you want to take your singing from the living room to outside audiences, you might begin in this way: I love to sing. I am a good singer, and I have music and words to share with many people. I will perform in a local open-mic by the end of the month. I will sing at two folk music festivals this summer. I will record a CD, and it will be successful.

Of course, your affirmations will follow your own talents and dreams.

51. The Unending Story

Do you remember the story of "Scheherazade" from the Arabian Nights? It is about a courageous young woman who had a plan to save many of the young women in the kingdom of one very twisted Sultan Schariar. He would take a new wife and, finding himself bored almost immediately, kill her and find another. Scheherazade married this misguided fellow and kept his interest by telling a story each night and ending it with the start of a new story. The Sultan was so curious about the latest cliffhanger that he kept his wife alive until, ultimately, her cleverness, beauty, and who knows what all, cured him of his homicidal tendencies. Of course, you are not at such risk, but here is a humble homage to brave Scheherazade.

When you come to the end of an essay, story, or poem, write three continuous free writes of five to ten minutes each. Begin with these prompts, but you may find some of your own that are better:

What happens next?
Then something appeared that changed everything.
That was just the beginning.

52. Charting the Flow

Chart the flow of a piece of writing, perhaps something that is giving you problems. Use your chart to show the ups and downs, the clarity, and the confusion. Does the plot or argument flow smoothly, transitioning naturally to new paragraphs, scenes, topics? What does your chart show about the writing?

53. Space

Open up your writing with sketches, doodle, paste some pictures in, add colors with markers or crayons, put in stage directions (now get up, go over to the window, scan the yard for two birds; or go outside the house and walk around the house twice; or meditate for five minutes; now go back to your story or essay). Tell the reader to listen for a cicada or cardinal, or put on some music.

Do this intermittently. Bring this active text into the writing, into the flow.

54. The Empty Vessel

We tend to forget that what we see in the media is representative of a minute part of this universe. In fact, it is a very small part of what is happening where the film or photograph was taken. First, it is a nanosecond in time and may or may not indicate much about what took place before and what will occur after. Second, the picture on the television screen and photograph are tightly constrained worlds. The most interesting, profound events are almost always outside those borders.

Look at a photograph from a newspaper or magazine. Describe what is going on outside the frame of the picture. For example, we see a crowd of apparently angry protesters carrying signs and raising their fists in defiance. Many people are behind the camera, over to the left in the park, sitting in their cars just out of view. What are they doing? Use your imagination to create possibilities.

This can also be done as you revise your own writing. Consider what is not being said, what is effectively between and behind the lines?

55. The Bisy Backson

We are almost all like Winnie the Pooh's Bisy Backson. We run around here and there doing this and that and rarely stopping to wonder why. We simply do not take the time to see the world and to question the need to be so busy. Here is an exercise in awareness:

Carry a small notepad with you all day long. In it, keep track of what you do throughout the day. Simply take the notebook out now and then, and jot down how you've spent the time since the last entry. At the end of the day, go back and underline or highlight everything that seems important. You'll be surprised at how much you resemble that Bisy Backson. Now, free write about the experience.

56. Tao Haiku

The Tao has a tradition of haiku, the Japanese art of spare, highly structured poetry. It is much like the tiny seed that contains a universe within it, so even though you may choose to write a haiku on a specifically Taoist theme, any haiku is a Taoist experience. This is a creative, pleasurable form of poetry. It can be fun, even silly, or it can be a way of expressing our deepest emotions and beliefs. Enjoy this activity.

The haiku has a rigid formula of three lines; the first and third lines have five syllables, the second line has seven syllables.

Here is an example:

Mountain rising up
Carrying earth on its back
Stone sings to the sky

Notice the number of syllables in each line. Here is a Japanese haiku:

> The sea at springtime
> all day it rises and falls,
> yes, rises and falls.
> —Buson

Select five to ten objects, scenes, or photographs, and create a haiku for each.

57. Heart-Song—the Rhythm of Your Heart

This is an activity that came to me one day as I listened to a young poet. As she spoke, I felt my heart beat in synch with her words.

Close your eyes and focus on the beat of your heart. Feel the rhythm pulse through you. Hear it in your mind and body. Begin to jot down any words that come to you as you are immersed in this heart-song. It may come out as a list of impressions, a poem, a lyrical story, or even a song lyric.

Here is an example of just such a heart-song:

> inside, inside
> as I am, as I am
> as I breathe, as I breathe
> as I live, as I live
> as I feel, as I feel
> as I hear, as I hear
> as I sing, as I sing
> as I am, as I am
> inside, inside

to my life, to my life
to my world, to my world
to my god, to my god
to my love, to my love
to my heart, to my heart
inside, inside, inside, inside
inside, inside, inside . . .

58. The Dream

We all dream, yet we forget most of these stories that run
through our night's sleep. However, we may find wonderfully
rich ideas in our dreams. Try this: for a week, keep a notebook
and pen at your bedside. When you awake in the night from a
dream, or first thing in the morning, write down your memories
of dreaming. These may be vivid blow-by-blow narratives, or
they may simply be impressions. At the end of the week, go
back and read what you have written. Look for a spark, something intriguing, a kernel of an idea, and free write on that idea
for fifteen or twenty minutes. Then write a scene or a poem
around the free write and the dream.

59. The Nightmare

Dreams are not always pleasant. In fact, as with many of our
waking experiences, we seem to remember the unpleasant
or traumatic events, even those we dream, far more vividly
than the good. Nightmares often confront our deepest fears
and concerns and, if we are lucky, give us a chance to work
through these fears. They also can provide us with powerful
inspiration for our creative sides. As the Tao reminds us, all is

not sweetness and light in the universe. The dark too is necessary and powerful.

Try this: Think back to a frightening or particularly troubling dream. Free write for twenty minutes abut this nightmare experience. After a short break, free write for another twenty minutes on confronting the fear or the demon at the heart of the dream (if you're comfortable with free writing, try extending the time). Use the power of your writing to create such light as to illuminate and thus dispel the darkness and vanquish these demons.

Now, write a poem expressing this cleansing experience.

Next, create a dream character. Give this person or creature a name and description. Then write a scene in which this character confronts a manifestation of the fear or evil represented in the dream. This activity gives great power to the writer. You may defeat the fear easily, or you may choose to make your protagonist work through complications and difficulties, through failure, to ultimately win out. The goal is that the evil be defeated.

In variation on this activity, the writer or protagonist becomes the demon in the story, in effect, confronting the fear from the inside out.

60. Chuang Chou's Butterfly

Emulate Chuang Tzu. Write for several minutes as if you were dreaming of being a butterfly. Then write for several minutes as if you were a butterfly dreaming of being a man or woman. Try this with other creatures, animals, insects, microbes; try it as a creature from mythology or fantasy: a dragon, fairy, alien, Banshee; then try it from the perspective of inanimate objects: a plant, a tree, a pebble, a mountain.

61. Dream Symbols

In the West the most common dream symbols are said to be these: kissing, water, nudity, money, losing something valuable or someone, flying, colors, running, sexual acts, and teeth. Free write on each of these. If something flows well for you explore it more fully in further free writing. Then create a poem, story, or essay based on the writing. Other archetypal dream symbols include the hero, magic, death, creation, demons, war, food, smoking, money, and many others. For more, you might search the Internet or look through the numerous books on the subject.

62. Focusing the Writer's Mind

If getting started is difficult, you can focus your writer's mind on an important question or concern. A clear lead-in can help. If you are having problems at work, you might begin with something like this: My job hasn't been very satisfying lately . . ., or People at work aren't getting along . . . . Then, simply keep writing. You may ask questions, explore alternatives, create fantasy solutions, or think on paper about your relationship to the problems. Other lead-in phrases can have to do with aspirations or values, and such: The thing I value most is . . .; Happiness is . . .; The best things about me are . . .; My dreams for the future are . . .; What's bothering me most is . . .

63. The I-Search

This exercise is based on the concept of the I-search research paper developed by Ken Macrorie in 1988. Since then, the I-search format has become popular in school and college writing classes, but it definitely should not be limited to school writing. I-search writing is a wonderful way to grow the seed of an idea into a wonderful, beautiful blossoming tree. Here is what you do:

Make a list entitled "Things I want to know more about." For example, you might jot down playing chess, dieting, painting in oils, Taoism, Buddha, Jesus, Mohammed, jazz, anger, running a marathon, raising chickens, writing my memoir, brewing beer, growing vegetables in the city, opera, toilet training, making kites, playing the banjo, NASCAR, or whatever else you fancy. You get the picture. Next, go through the list, and choose something you hope to explore further. Now, for the I-search process:

- At the top of a piece of paper, write out everything you can think of about your subject—what you know, what you have heard and believe, and what you think may be true.
- Next, at the top of a piece of paper, write "This is what I want to know, or learn, about_____." Again, go into as much detail as possible.
- Now, write as succinctly as possible, "I want to explore _____ because . . ."

At the top of a page write "The Search." Now begin looking for information, collecting data, discovering the answers to your questions, and as you embark on this hunt, write its story. Tell what you did, what failed, what succeeded, and why.

- Take a new piece of paper. At the top write, "This is what I discovered." Narrate your conclusions in this section.
- Finally, begin a page with this heading: "Where do I go from here?" This is where you talk about new questions

that have arisen and the next steps you might take. For example, after you've learned about materials, techniques, and instruction in pottery, you might just go out and join a pottery class.

The I-search is enough in itself, but it can also be a stepping-stone to a more polished piece of writing. Rewrite your I-search in the third person as an article, or even the beginning of a book. You might choose a more formal voice here. Or, rewrite the I-search as a nonfiction narrative. Tell the story through the voice and point of view of a unique character, as if it were fiction.

The I-search form can go as far as you want to take it.

64. Self-discovery

Create a character who is like you. Then write a scene in which you transform him or her through an author's kind of alchemy. The character might peel away your skin to reveal something or somebody altogether different. Include a deep transformation until there is a dramatic metamorphosis, and the character is no longer you. Then go back and replant bits of yourself in your character, not a lot, just enough to make him or her interesting. Other ways of transforming this "I" character might take place through a literal rebirth, or it might be a Dr. Jekyll and Mr. Hyde kind of shape-shifting. In the end, your anti-you character may seem to be your opposite, but is, in fact, more likely to reflect your alter ego, even your darker self. Write a short story around this character.

65. Inner Search

Imagine you are on a search, a search for yourself. Write a narrative of the search. Where do you find you? Describe in detail the path to finding this objective. How do you feel when you first encounter yourself? Who you are, and what you do. What happens when you first encounter yourself? What happens after that?

66. Creation and Destruction

Write a poem entitled "This Poem is Gone." Then, let go of it— burn it, bury it, soak it in water until it is merely pulp again— delete it, paint over it—use your imagination, and make it disappear.

67. Eternity

For a few moments breathe calmly and consciously. Then, imagine that in exhaling, your breath flows out into the air, into the world, beyond the atmosphere and into the universe, and goes on and on. Write a passage describing this great, eternal exhalation. Evoke the flow, the energy, and the movement of one human breath. Think about the very personal nature of the act of breathing. Think about the blending of human breath, the great blending of exhalations in time and space.

Now, write the journey, the adventure of one breath.

68. The Eternal Poem

In the evening, just before going to bed, write a poem. Put it aside. The next night, read this evening poem and use the last line to begin a second poem. Again, put it aside until the following evening, and take the last line of this poem and begin a third. Do this for a week, a month, a year, or longer. An alternative is to write one poem a week based on the last line of the last poem.

69. Sharing the Spirit

Create a Web page of interests, essays, poems, and stories. Share it with friends, or share it with the whole Internet.

70. Writing the Tao

Writing teachers often use prompts to get students moving, to prime the writing pump, so to speak. Although it may seem that a prescribed prompt can stifle originality, in fact the opposite seems to be true. One of my favorite prompts, "I never told this to anyone . . ." has given rise to a remarkable variety and range of writing among my students.

For this activity, choose a passage or line from the Tao Te Ching. Write it down, and, taking your cue from the line, begin writing. There is no right or wrong passage, and whatever you may write is the right thing.

Here are some of my favorite bits from the Tao:

The best of man is like water . . . (verse 8)
Too much play maddens the mind. (verse 12)
Too much desire tears the heart. (verse 12)
Those who wish to change the world, according to their desire, cannot succeed. (verse 29)
Without looking through the window, you may see the ways of heaven. (verse 47)

Bibliography

Abbey, Edward. *Desert Solitaire: A Season in the Wilderness.* New York: Random House, 1968.

Batcheller, Lori. "Journal Keeping: A Place for Healing, Self-Discovery, and Creative Flow." *www.byregion.net/articles-healers/journaling.html.*

Belanoff, Pat, Peter Elbow, and Sheryl I. Fontaine, eds. *Nothing Begins with N: New Investigations of Freewriting.* Carbondale, Illinois: Southern Illinois University Press, 1991.

Borkin, Susan. *When Your Heart Speaks, Take Good Notes: The Healing Power of Writing.* Center for Personal Growth: 2000. (an excerpt from *www.susanborkin.com/excerpt_tao_of_writing.htm*).

Bradbury, Ray. *Zen in the Art of Writing: Lessons on Creativity.* Santa Barbara: Capra Press, 1990.

Buehler, Georg. "Seekers Wanted, Apply Within: Finding a Livelihood for the Modern Spiritual Life." In "Radical Spirit: Spiritual Writings from the Voices for Tomorrow."

Stephen Dinan, ed. Novato, California: New World Library, 2002.

Burke, Patricia A. "A Writing Meditation." *www.patriciaburke.com/writingmeditation.html.*

Calkins, Lucy. *The Art of Teaching Writing.* New York: Heinemann, 1994.

Castaneda, Carlos. *Journey to Ixtlan: The Lessons of Don Juan.* New York: Pocket Books, 1972.

Chinese Character Dictionary: *http://chinalanguage.com/CCDICT/.*

Chuang Tzu. *The Essential Chuang Tzu.* Sam Hamill and J. P. Seaton, trans. and eds. Boston: Shambhala, 1998.

Chung, Douglas K. "Taoism: A Portrait." *A Sourcebook for Earth's Community of Religions.* New York: Global Education Associates, 1995. *www.silcom.com/~origin/sbcr/taoism.htm.*

Collins, Terah Katherine. *The Western Guide to Feng Shui.* Carlsbad, California: Hay House, 1996.

Cortwright, Susie Michelle. "Journaling: A Tool for the Spirit." *www.jennibick.com/tool-for-spirit.html.*

Csikszentmihalyi, Mihaly. *Creativity: Flow and the Psychology of Discovery and Invention*. New York: Harper Collins, 1996.

Dalai Lama. *A Human Approach to World Peace*. DharmaNet ed. Berkeley, California: DharmaNet, 1994. *www.sacredtexts.com/bud/tib/humpeace.htm*. Accessed March 2005.

Dreher, Diane. *The Tao of Inner Peace*. New York: Harper Collins, 1990.

Elbow, Peter. *Writing with Power: Techniques for Mastering the Writing Process*. New York: Oxford University Press, 1998.

Freire, Paulo. *Education for Critical Consciousness*. New York: Continuum Publishing Co., 1992.

Gleick, James. *The Genius and Life of Richard Feynman*. New York: Random House, 1992.

Goldberg, Natalie. *Writing Down the Bones: Freeing the Writer Within*. New York: Shambhala, 1986.

Hairston, Maxine, and Michael Keene. *Successful Writing*. 5th ed. New York: W. W. Norton and Co., 2003.

Hamill, Sam, and J. P. Seaton, eds. *The Essential Chuang Tzu*. Boston: Shambhala, 1999.

Heider, John. *The Tao of Leadership*. New York: Bantam, 1986.

Hoff, Benjamin. The Tao of Pooh. New York: Penguin Books, 1982.

Jacobs, William Wymark. "The Monkey's Paw." (The story first appeared in *Harper's Monthly* magazine in 1902 and was reprinted in his third collection of short stories, *The Lady of the Barge*.) New York: Harper & Brothers, Publishers, 1902. In my teaching I access the story at this Web site: *http://gaslight.mtroyal.ca/mnkyspaw.htm*.

Kardash, Ted. "Taoism—Ageless Wisdom for a Modern World: Te—The Principle of Inner Nature." *www.jade dragon.com/archives/april98/tao.html*. April 1998. Accessed November 2002.

Kornfield, Jack, ed. *Teachings of the Buddha*. Boston: Shambhala, 1993.

Krementz, Jill. *The Writer's Desk*. New York: Random House, Inc., 1996.

Lao Tzu. *Tao Te Ching*. Gia Fu-Feng and Jane English, trans. New York: Vintage Books, 1989.

Lao Tzu. *Tao Te Ching*. J. Legge, trans. Internet Sacred Text Archive. www.sacred-texts.com/tao/taote.htm.

Lao Tzu. *The Way of Life: Tao Te Ching*. R.B. Blakney, trans. New York: Penguin Putnam Inc., 1983.

Liu, Xiaogan. "Naturalness (Tzu-jan), the Core Value in Taoism: Its Ancient Meaning and Its Significance Today." In *Lao Tzu and the Tao-te-ching*. Livia Kohn and Michael LaFargue, eds. Albany: State University of New York Press, 1998.

London, Jack. *White Fang*. London: Puffin Books, 1994. First published in the *Strand* magazine in 1905.

Maclean, Norman. *A River Runs Through It*. New York: Pocket Books, 1976.

Macrorie, Ken. *The I-Search Paper*. Portsmouth, New Hampshire: Boynton/Cook Publishers, 1988.

Milner, Marion (Joanna Field). *On Not Being Able to Paint*. New York: International Universities Press, 1957.

Olson, D. R. "From Utterance to Text." *In Perspectives on Literacy*. E. R. Kintgen, B. M. Kroll, and M. Rose, eds. Carbondale, Illinois: Southern Illinois University Press, 1988. pp. 175–189.

Olswanger, Anna. "Writing as an Act of Discovery: A Conversation with Juanita Havill." *www.underdown.org/havill.htm*. Accessed June 2004.

Osho. *Creativity: Unleashing the Forces Within*. New York: St. Martins Press, 1999.

Paine, Thomas. "The Crisis." Pamphlet, published in 1776. In my classes, I access "The Crisis" at www.ushistory.org/paine/crisis/c-01.htm.

Perry, Susan K. *Writing in Flow: Keys to Enhanced Creativity*. Cincinnati: Writer's Digest Books, 1999.

Roy, Arundhati. *The God of Small Things*. New York: Harper Collins, 1998.

Shaughnessy, Mina. *Errors and Expectations*. New York: Oxford University Press, 1977.

Simpkins, Alexander C., and Annellen M. Simpkins. *Living Meditation from Principle to Practice*. Boston: Tuttle Publishing, 1997.

Stevenson, Robert Louis. *The Strange Case of Dr. Jekyll and Mister Hyde*. New York: Bantam, 1981.

Too, Lillian. *The Fundamentals of Feng Shui*. Boston: Element Books, 1999.

Toole, John Kennedy. *A Confederacy of Dunces*. New York: Random House, Inc., 1980.

Wahlstrom, Ralph L. "Getting Burned." *Ellery Queen's Mystery Magazine*, February 1984.

Wahlstrom, Ralph L. "The Keening Woods." *Above the Bridge*. May–June 1988.

Walker, Brian, ed. *Hua Hu Ching: The Unknown Teachings of Lao Tzu*. San Francisco: Harper, 1992.

Webster, Richard. *101 Feng Shui Tips*. St. Paul: Llewellyn, 1998.

Zemelman, Steven, and Harvey Daniels. *A Community of Writers: Teaching Writing in the Junior and Senior High School*. Portsmouth, New Hampshire: Heinemann, 1988.

Zenith, Steven Ericsson, ed. "The Simple Way of Lao Tzu." *www.wingchun.dk/library/laotzu/tao.te.ching.aspx*.

Zinsser, William. *On Writing Well, 25th Anniversary Edition*. New York: Harper Collins, 2001.

Zinsser, William. *Writing to Learn*. New York: Harper & Row, 1988.